# WORLD
## NEWS GROUP

Gary,

One of my favorite movie dialogues comes in *Blackhawk Down*, a film set in 1993 Somalia. U.S. soldiers are in a life-or-death struggle. A colonel tells a bleeding sergeant, "Get in that truck and drive." The sergeant responds, "But I'm shot." The colonel barks back, "Everybody's been shot. Get in and drive."

Some of us when growing up had the blessing of great fathers. Others did not. I was shot, and only recently have learned to honor my father. I poured my heart into the enclosed book, and want to thank you and other generous donors for pouring support into WORLD.

I hope *Lament for a Father* will be useful to you or someone you love.

Marvin

After spending more than forty years with Marvin Olasky the journalist, I needed this great little book to discover several other facets to his colorful persona. There are no "bare facts" in this man's life. Everything is part of a sovereign design.
—**Joel Belz**, Founder, *World* magazine

What is Marvin Olasky's *Lament for a Father*? Is it a tracing of the plummet of twentieth-century intellectual life into eugenics and anti-Semitism? Is it the chronicle of Jewish suffering in World War II? Is it a critique of the secularization of American society and education? Is it an attempt to understand the psychology of how brutality passes from generation to generation? Is it a son's attempt to understand the dysfunction of his parents' deeply unhappy marriage, his father's failure, and his mother's scorn? Is it the story of a broken actor on a broken stage? It is all of these, but ultimately it is one man's agonizingly circuitous journey to faith in Christ, to gratitude, and finally to honoring a tragically flawed and tormented father.
—**Douglas Bond**, Author, *Stand Fast in the Way of Truth*
    (Fathers & Sons)

Marvin Olasky walks readers through the process of understanding his father's world and in the process teaches all to do the same with our own fathers. With a posture of compassion, grace, and mercy, *Lament for a Father* puts on display what happens when the gospel shapes the way we remember our fathers and gives us permission to experience the joy and pain of imperfection. Olasky shows us how researching our parents' past can lead to a place of healing and reconciliation. It's an extraordinary testimony to the all too common brokenness of the families of World War II combat veterans that shaped the generation after them. It's a riveting tale.
—**Anthony B. Bradley**, Professor of Religious Studies, The
    King's College; Director, The Center for the Study of Human
    Flourishing

For decades, few voices have been more important in the American church than that of Marvin Olasky, as he has shaped a generation of Christians to apply the good news of the gospel toward the flourishing of healthy communities. But in this book, Marvin pulls back the layers of his own storied life, one that itself is a dramatic tale of God's saving grace. Olasky allows us to see the story behind the sage, sharing for the first time his difficult relationship with his father, sharing in emotional and poignant words the aching longing in his heart for the father who could have been and the satisfaction he has found in the Father he knows. Every human being, no matter how accomplished, wants to know and be known by their dads. Pick up this book, read it, and buy an extra copy for a friend who needs to read it. You will not be disappointed.

—**Daniel Darling**, Senior Vice President, NRB; Best-Selling Author, *A Way with Words*, *The Dignity Revolution*, and *The Characters of Christmas*

Marvin Olasky is an extraordinarily gifted man: a journalist, editor, professor, theologian, and writer with a talent for doing relentless research. In this book, he turns his microscope on a man he didn't like, who disappointed him and failed him, a man he wanted to admire but couldn't: Eli Olasky, his father. Eli graduated from Harvard, a brilliant man with scholarly ambitions, but after returning from military service at the end of World War II, he drifted from job to job and became a stoic who never laughed or played baseball with his son. Why? What happened? It's a gripping story about family, faith, suffering, and forgiveness. A true lament.

—**John R. Erickson**, Author, Hank the Cowdog series

Marvin Olasky explains how he finally came to understand, appreciate, and forgive his brilliant but emotionally distant and underachieving father who died in 1984. Through painstaking but fascinating historical research, Olasky comes to understand

his father's difficult life as he grew up as a young boy in a Jewish immigrant community in early twentieth-century Boston and then experienced debilitating stress as a US Army soldier assigned to help to clean out the horrible remains of Nazi atrocities in Jewish death camps at the end of World War II. Olasky has written this book not only to honor his father's memory but also to explain how he himself changed from an atheistic, zealous communist to a born-again evangelical Christian who has edited *World* magazine for the past three decades. Anyone who has experienced a difficult parent-child relationship will appreciate the wisdom in this book.
—**Wayne Grudem**, Distinguished Research Professor of
  Theology and Biblical Studies, Phoenix Seminary

Marvin Olasky has been an intellectual, theological, and economic treasure for decades. In *Lament for a Father*, he serves up a poignant, intimate, and engaging memoir crammed full of lessons about what makes for manhood with honest meditations on themes ranging from anti-Semitism to redemption. Beware: this book is addictive.
—**Robert A. Sirico**, Founder, Acton Institute

I first discovered Marvin Olasky through his book *The Tragedy of American Compassion*, which told the history of faith-based charities designed to lift people out of poverty by transforming their lives, not sustaining them in poverty. Newt Gingrich, the future speaker of the House, was so impressed that he bought copies to distribute to his fellow members of Congress. In his latest book, *Lament for a Father*, Marvin takes us through the early part of his life in ways that sound depressing until you get to the end. As a brilliant writer and thinker, Marvin consoles those who have had difficult parents and shows through his own experience they do not have to determine the course of the lives of their children.
—**Cal Thomas**, Syndicated Columnist

A sense of longing and loss pervades Marvin Olasky's tribute to his father—a reckoning with his Jewish heritage that remains sensitive to time and culture, faith and freedom. A beautiful lament suffused with gratitude and honor.
—**Trevin Wax**, Author, *Rethink Your Self, This Is Our Time*, and *Gospel-Centered Teaching*

Marvin Olasky's memoir of his quest to understand his inscrutable father whisked me from working class New England to the brutal execution of his Russian great-grandparents to the concentration camps of the Third Reich. With the diligence of a journalist and the penitent longing of an errant son, Olasky digs up his father's past to learn what changed him from a passionate scholar to a remote stoic whose wife called him "lazy and lacking ambition." The result is a vividly drawn journey during which Olasky exchanges scorn for honor and bitterness for grace. *Lament for a Father* is a poignant reminder that even our most deeply rooted family resentments can be gloriously and unexpectedly redeemed.
—**Lynn Vincent**, *New York Times* Best-Selling Author; Investigative Journalist; Navy Veteran

In this accessible true-life tale, Marvin Olasky truly fathoms his father for the first time, uncovering a loss of faith in God that led to a collapse of faith in self and eventually an evaporation of all confidence in the promise of life. It's a searing, unblinkingly honest, yet ultimately consoling story of family life, ethnicity, and growing up, capped by an engrossing appendix in which the author describes his own recovery of faith.
—**Karl Zinsmeister**, Author; Journalist; Consultant

# Lament
## *for a*
# Father

The Journey to Understanding
and Forgiveness

# Marvin Olasky

**P&R**
**P U B L I S H I N G**
P.O. BOX 817 • PHILLIPSBURG • NEW JERSEY 08865-0817

Printed in the United States of America

**Library of Congress Cataloging-in-Publication Data**

Names: Olasky, Marvin N., author.
Title: Lament for a father : the journey to understanding and forgiveness / Marvin Olasky.
Description: Phillipsburg, New Jersey : P&R Publishing, [2021] | Includes bibliographical references. | Summary: "Marvin Olasky explores how his Jewish American father was impacted by World War II, Reconstructionist Judaism, and social Darwinist teaching at Harvard-facing pain in order to understand and forgive"-- Provided by publisher.
Identifiers: LCCN 2021008273 | ISBN 9781629958668 (paperback) | ISBN 9781629958675 (epub) | ISBN 9781629958682 (mobi)
Subjects: LCSH: Olasky, Eli, 1917-1984. | Jewish educators--United States--Biography. | Husband and wife--United States. | Fathers and sons--United States. | Forgiveness--Religious aspects. | Olasky, Marvin N.
Classification: LCC BM102.O43 O43 2021 | DDC 296.092 [B]--dc23
LC record available at https://lccn.loc.gov/2021008273

Here's a dictionary definition: "A book dedication is a way for an author to honor a person (or group of people)."

So in one sense I'm dedicating this book to my father, who's the main character in it. But I'm also taking the unusual step of dedicating it to you, the reader. You may be looking at this page right now because you have unresolved conflicts with a parent, living or dead. You deserve more than to go through the rest of your life feeling either guilty or angry.

I wrote this to blaze a trail through my own forest, and to encourage you to do likewise.

# Contents

Introduction    7

1. Memories    11
2. "Lazy and Lacking Ambition"    21
3. One Shining Moment    35
4. Seeing the Worst    47
5. Someone to Watch over Me    59
6. It's an Unrespected Life    69
7. The Unkindest Cuts of All    81
8. Beyond Scapegoats    93

Appendix: How God Saved Me    107
Partial Bibliography    113

# Introduction

I've watched many times *Field of Dreams*, the 1989 movie starring Kevin Costner. Flawed though the film is, it always chokes me up. Although called "a baseball flick," the underlying motif is father-son relationships. At the end, Costner's character asks his dad, "You wanna have a catch?"

My lifetime catches with my father: zero. He has no interest in baseball. I never play until I'm eleven, when I'm a fat kid with a lazy left eye. My batting average during one year of Little League is .182, if I generously count as hits what are probably errors.

Still, I want to be at least a decent fielder. I nag my father to come out on the street and throw me some ground balls. I say "street" because we live on the second floor of an apartment in urban Massachusetts with no backyard or nearby green space. That means a missed ball goes rolling and rolling. That geography contributes to a missed opportunity.

One day, finally, my father agrees. We stand in front of the house. I walk twenty yards away. He throws me a ball that bounces twice before it should have hit my glove. I miss it. Embarrassed, and blaming my father rather than myself, I run after it and yell over my shoulder, "Why didn't you throw it straight?"

When I pick up the ball and turn around, he is walking up the steps to our front door. He goes inside. That's it. We never again even start a catch. Nor do we talk much. Once I become a teenager, we speak hardly at all.

Cut to October 1984. I'm thirty-four. He's sixty-seven—and dying of bladder cancer. I live two thousand miles away and fly to Boston with the public goal of providing some comfort and help. My private motive is selfish: to learn why he moved from ambitious youth just before World War II to decades of postwar failure, at least in the eyes of my mother, my brother, and me.

One evening we sit on a Danish modern couch in their apartment. He tells me some stories about his life in the 1930s and 1940s. Then I throw him a question about his dropping out of graduate school. The question is harder and curvier than a polite inquiry should have been. He gets up and walks away, saying over his shoulder, "Why don't you mind your own business?"

I put away the conversational ball and go to sleep. The next day I ask no more questions. My parents drive me to Boston's Logan Airport. He wears a baseball cap because chemotherapy has left him bald. I pull my suitcase out of the trunk, shake his hand, lean over, and whisper in his ear, "I love you," because that seems the right thing to say to a dying parent.

I never see him again. I wish I had persisted in my questioning about turning points in his past, both for true love and to gain true family history. In *Field of Dreams*, the son and the dad finally have a catch. That catches my tears, every time.

It catches other tears as well. After I write a *World* column about *Field of Dreams* and my own experience, letters from readers flow in. A typical comment: "My dad never, and I mean never, played anything with my brother or me. I deeply regret what I lost not having memories of my dad taking time to play with me." Another writes, "I know the great black hole that remains when a father is present and willfully absent at the same time. We finally walk away and begin the search for a Heavenly Father."

Jeffrey Munroe in *Reading Buechner*, a biography of the Christian author, focuses on the day in 1936 when Buechner's father deliberately "breathed in the carbon monoxide that killed him." Munroe says, "Buechner's life and career have been a quest to understand the meaning of that event and to understand where God was when the unthinkable happened."

The result is not so dramatic when a father is simultaneously present and absent, but many people judging by those letters—have unresolved conflicts with dads, living or dead. So do I. My father, born in 1917, graduates from Harvard in 1940 with great opportunities, only to give up his hopes sometime in the 1940s or 1950s. He suffers a spiritual and psychological death until his physical demise in 1984. Why?

Now that I'm seventy, why bother to look backward? Buechner says he deals "with the sad parts of [his] life by forgetting them." He writes, "I didn't know I was forgetting them . . . but the mechanism of forgetting had been so strongly switched on in my childhood that it became a sort of automatic response." He then discusses Jesus's parable of the talents, where two men who receive a lot of money use it to gain more, but the third, who receives a little, hides it in the ground.

Jesus chastises that third man, as does Buechner, who says such burial is "not really being alive. Not really making use of what happens to you. If you bury your life—if you don't face, among other things, your pain—your life shrinks."

I sometimes speak directly to the readers of *World*: After editing the magazine for almost thirty years, I feel like I know them. I don't know who will read this book, but I'd like the liberty now to speak directly to them—I mean you. Since I want to be forgiven for my trespasses, I need to forgive the trespasses of others. So do you, if you still have regrets regarding your interaction with your father. Or so does someone you love.

My first piece of advice is to do what I did not do: Persist in questioning while your father is still alive. Don't take no for a final answer. Learn about your father's life. If he won't tell all or anything, at least ask about his parents and grandparents. And here's my second piece, based on what I've learned in writing this book: even if it seems too late, it's not.

Here's some of my research path: Interview ten cousins for information about our grandparents and their impressions of my father. Buy a membership in Ancestry.com and find the naturalization papers of one grandfather and the marriage records of the other. Roam the internet to learn details of life in the 1930s and 1940s: Metropolitan Opera broadcast schedules, neighborhood activities, Harvard graduate courses, trolley and subway maps, hit songs and radio broadcast times in the 1940s.

I've written many history books, of course using the past tense to write about the past. But this book is different. The research has made my father come alive to me, so the past seems like the present, and I've taken the unusual tack of writing almost entirely in the present tense.

I understand more about my father, now that I know about his experiences. I understand my mother more. You can make your parents and grandparents come more alive to you—you just have to dig in. This book shows what I now know, but it also points the way to what you can learn.

# 1

# Memories

In 1956 we live in a four-room apartment on the third floor of a triple-decker in Malden, Massachusetts, just north of Boston. Ward Seven is mostly Jewish and working class, with rows of wooden houses containing one apartment per floor. Our living room has comfortable but mismatched dark furniture: dark green couch, brown wingback chair, a plain wooden rocking chair. The floor and windows have lighter colors: an orange oval-shaped throw rug in the middle, beige window shades that I like to pull up and down by a string with a looped end. We have radiators for warmth and open windows for cooling.

No one speaks much. We don't yet have a television. I'm six. My brother Sidney is nine. He teaches me to play chess. We play in the evening while lying on the rug, propped up by our elbows. I've learned how to read by ingesting Classics Illustrated comic books that cost fifteen cents and include *Moby Dick* (no. 16), *Robin Hood* (no. 3), and *Don Quixote* (no. 11). My father, Eli Olasky, sits in the wingback chair reading science fiction or mystery stories, little paperbacks with the covers torn off so they could be sold for a nickel. Sometimes he takes out heavy books with letters not in English and reads from right to left.

Three introverted males reading or playing chess, in silence befitting a Trappist monastery. Into the room lopes my thin and dark-haired mother, who wants to see the world but is now stuck in an apartment half a mile from where she grew up. At age six I miss subtle signs of marital discord, but it's hard to mistake misery when she periodically screams, *Harvard man! Lazy! No ambition! Why don't we have a house! Why don't we go anywhere?* My father walks into their bedroom and closes the door. Sometimes my mother goes after him.

On Saturday mornings Sidney walks to the synagogue with our father. They then walk to our grandfather's house for a Sabbath dinner. Our mother does not go to the synagogue or to dinner. I, a fat child with little legs, stay with her in the kitchen. It features a sink mounted to the wall, a curved-top refrigerator that requires periodic defrosting, a free-standing cupboard with separate meat and milk dishes, and a gas range.

After lunch, which typically emerges from cans of tuna fish, peas, and carrots, I sit at a rectangular table with room for four and a plastic laminate surface. My mother turns on the Texaco Metropolitan Opera broadcasts and listens while she dusts, washes dishes, mops the linoleum floor, and strides back and forth, sometimes peering out the small window.

My job is to listen to my mother between acts. She tells me I am lucky to have a bed of my own in a room I share with Sidney: she had to sleep with either an older sister or an aunt. I am lucky to have a teddy bear: she never had a doll or a stuffed animal. I am lucky because someday I will go to college: she was smart and worked hard in school but never had the opportunity. I am not lucky to live in an apartment with peeling linoleum and scratched wooden floors. My aunts and uncles walk barefoot on "wall-to-wall carpet."

Then the next act begins. Sometimes I ask my mother what the story is about. She tells me in a sentence. It's always bad news for the principal woman. In *Lucia di Lammermoor*, Lucia knifes her bridegroom and dies in front of wedding guests. In *Aida* and *Madame Butterfly*, the title characters commit suicide. José kills Carmen in the opera with her name on it. Gilda in *Rigoletto* dies at the hands of a hit man her father hired. Leonara in *Il Trovatore* swallows poison to avoid rape. Mimì in *La Bohème* and Violetta in *La Traviata* die of tuberculosis.

I can see my mother is sad, so I try to amuse her by looking at a book or a magazine and finding a big word I don't know. I try to pronounce it. When she cries, I ask her for three-digit numbers, add them in my head, and yell the answer like a stand-up comic desperately trying to wring smiles from a cranky audience. My wages are a plate of Fig Newtons and a glass of Nestle's Quik, heavy on the chocolate powder.

Every other Sunday evening my parents play bridge with my mother's five brothers and sisters, each with a spouse. They rotate from house to house: when it's our turn, the twelve adults sit in groups of four around three card tables. They all smoke cigarettes or cigars. My aunts notice what clothes others are wearing. If something is new, my mother asks, "What's something like that cost?" or "Where did you buy it?" Her tone, often accusatory, forces the offending sister to say, "I spent too much." That means she can afford to spend too much, which my mother can't.

As the card playing begins, aunts and uncles try to engage my father in small talk: "Seen any movies you like?" He stares at the chatterer and says, "Let's pay attention to our cards." He reads books about bridge strategy and knows that 999 of 1,000 times a bridge hand has a card higher than a nine. He points out the mistakes in bidding others make. The uncles tell jokes and roar with laughter. As both my brother and I remember, our father never laughs.

I enjoy most about those evenings the opportunity to show off. My mother talks about how smart her children are: I can say the alphabet backward. An aunt or uncle calls to me, "Mahvin, show us what you can do." I stand proudly in my plaid knee-length shorts, my belly pushing against the fabric of my button-up shirt. Dark socks and dark leather shoes finish the look as I rapid-fire announce, "Z-Y-X-W-V-U-T-S . . ." and go all the way to "C-B-A," in a rush. The grown-ups applaud and hand me Brach's sugared fruit slices, M&M's King Size peanuts, and Tootsie Rolls.

In 1957 we drive down US Route 1 to Hollywood, Florida, where my father will be the principal of a Hebrew school that students attend after public school lets out. One night we eat at a Howard Johnson's. The table looks a lot like the one we have at home, with the same laminate surface. My father orders a hamburger and a wedge of iceberg lettuce. No ketchup or mustard on the burger. No dressing on the non-salad salad. My mother orders beef burgundy.

I request a small wedge of lettuce and a child's hamburger. Since we eat only kosher meat at home, I ask the waitress if it's kosher. She laughs and walks away. My father says it isn't. I ask, "Why are we eating it?" He says, "It's not important." My mother takes one forkful of beef burgundy and waves her hand to summon the waitress. She tells her, "It's undercooked." That's true. All the meat we eat at home is in the oven so long that hamburgers look like the eight balls I once saw. By the time the waitress brings back the beef burgundy, the rest of us have finished eating. My mother complains to the waitress again. The manager comes back and gives my brother and me free desserts, vanilla ice cream with lots of chocolate sauce.

In Florida I glory in my father being a principal, which means he's the most important person, not just someone screamed at. He knows so much. He knows the frequency distribution of English letters: E most often, but people who think the other vowels follow immediately are wrong. (T, A, O, and N came next.) But he does not love talking to parents or to his school board. My mother's tirades become more specific: "You just want to read. Why don't you schmooze with them?"

The Atlantic Ocean is only two miles away, so we go to the beach, once. We spread a blanket on the sand. After a few minutes my mother jumps up and runs away with a cloud of gnats behind her. She says Revere Beach north of Boston is better, even though when we go there once my brother and I have to wear our Keds in the ocean because we "might step on a broken bottle."

Our house in Florida has 980 square feet and lacks air conditioning, but it has jalousie windows, glass slats that I crank up and down. One time I'm hot in the middle of the night. I rise to open our living room windows, closed to protect against robbers. My mother is also up, throwing shoes at palmetto bugs (a.k.a., giant cockroaches) scampering across the wooden floor.

In 1959 we suddenly drive back north to Massachusetts. I now know some American history and desperately want to stop in Washington, DC, to see the Capitol and the White House. My father says, "It's not important." We bypass them. We stay temporarily at the home of my grandfather, Louis Olasky. I watch him pray in the morning. He fastens to his

arms and forehead a deeply worn set of black straps and little black boxes. I ask my father why he doesn't put on those
things. He says, "I'm not Orthodox like my father." That
doesn't satisfy me. "But why?" He says it's not important.

As Christmas approaches, my fourth-grade public
school class has the task of putting on the back wall of our
schoolroom a paper mosaic of a nativity scene. The teacher
assigns me to help to make the baby Jesus. In a spurt of
hyper-Orthodoxy, I refuse, telling the principal, "If I don't
believe this, why should I do it?" My father says, "It's not
important." He brokers a compromise: I will work only on
nonreligious parts of the mosaic. For the next week, I reluc-
tantly spend art period cutting out white bits of paper that
form the snow of a wintry scene.

By that time, we have a black-and-white television. I start
watching Westerns: In the fall of 1959, prime time on television features twenty-six, including eight of the ten most-
watched shows according to Nielsen ratings. My favorite is
*The Rifleman*, the first television series to have a widowed
father raising a son. The star, Chuck Connors, played in
the NBA for the Boston Celtics in 1946: he was the first
professional basketball player to shatter a glass backboard.
On television he expertly handles a Winchester rifle with a
modified trigger mechanism that allows for rapid-fire shots!
During the opening credits each week Connors says, "A man
doesn't run from a fight."

The other Western I watch is *Have Gun, Will Travel*, which
debuts in 1957 and ranks fourth in the Nielsen ratings
during its first four years. The star, Richard Boone, is not
conventionally handsome. He has a wisp of a mustache like
the one my father sometimes sports. He has a pockmarked
face, and—most important—a nose that makes me wonder,

Could he be Jewish? (I later find out he is, or his mother was, which is officially good enough.)

Boone's character, Paladin, is ready to kill when necessary but prefers books and chess. He is obviously smart: I later hear screenwriter Sam Rolfe saying the success of the show hinges on Boone's ability to "play a high-IQ gunslinger and get away with it." Paladin quotes Shakespeare. (For the benefit of nine-year-olds, someone says, "That's Shakespeare, ain't it?") He drops so many references to Aristotle that one TV critic exults, "Where else can you see a gun fight and absorb a classical education at the same time?" Paladin is my hero. And he doesn't exist.

Those are my main childhood memories. I also remember names of a few prominent individuals my father mentions admiringly. David Ben-Gurion, the first prime minister of Israel. Henry Wallace, the US vice president in the early 1940s. Theologian Mordecai Kaplan.

When I become a teenager, I no longer admire my father, but I do admire two of his possessions: a mahogany four-drawer filing cabinet and a mahogany four-shelf bookcase. They aren't mismatched pieces like our other furniture: they make up an elegant set, and the drawers on the filing cabinet roll with exceptional smoothness.

One afternoon I try to rummage through the filing cabinet, but it's locked. After my father dies of cancer, my mother throws out its contents. All I remember of the bookcase's contents: several books by Kaplan, along with the classic *Meditations* of Stoic Marcus Aurelius. My father channeled that stoicism into the advice he offered others: "Expect the worst, so you won't be disappointed."

My mother expects the worst, but she is still disappointed. Here's one example: In 1965 my parents, my brother, and

I go to my father's twenty-fifth reunion and sleep for two nights in a Harvard dorm suite. My father surprises me by saying this is the first night he has ever spent in a dorm there. My mother says she wants to sip sherry in a Harvard master's home and sit in a seminar. If she does, she goes alone, because my father goes to sit in Widener Library: "I never got to use it much."

The *New York Times* reports that the reunion features "handshakes, talking, and laughter. But the man who would have made the difference for the class of 1940 was absent." I ask my father about that, and he surprises me by heatedly responding, "Kennedy was a faker. He didn't even write his own senior thesis."

My father refuses to go to the Essex County Country Club for a class picnic, and my mother surprisingly doesn't demand that: "We don't have the right clothes." I roam Harvard Square, and when I return, she walks once more on some well-trod territory: "Your father could have done so much, but he lacked ambition. I tried to help him achieve what he was capable of achieving. Do you know why he developed an escapist personality?" I say I do not know and leave the room.

Massachusetts is having a heat wave on those June days, but for some reason the heat in our suite comes on that night and we cannot stop it. My mother says she can't stand such a roasting. She tries unsuccessfully to find a janitor. She comes back muttering about how she's almost always unlucky.

"But there was one time," she says, and tells a story about November 28, 1942. A wealthy boyfriend drives her to one of downtown Boston's premier nightclubs, the Cocoanut Grove. The Grove has columns that look like palm trees with light fixtures made to look like cocoanuts.

Dark blue satin covers the ceilings, bamboo and rattan the walls. Drapes conceal exits.

That night, though, she and her date cannot get in because the nightclub, with an official capacity of 460, already has one thousand people inside. Later, a fire breaks out and spreads rapidly. Patrons crawl through thick clouds of smoke. Bodies pile up at a jammed revolving door. Some that open inward do not open at all when dozens of people press against them. The death toll is 492, making it the deadliest nightclub fire ever.

My mother says, "The best thing in my life was not being in that fire."

In 2008, when my mother is dying, I start slowly filling a filing cabinet drawer with facts and stories gained from her and from my brother and cousins—sometimes their own observations, sometimes things my father told them. From their memories I've reconstructed scenes and conversations, keeping in mind characterizations like this one from a cousin about my mother: "The angriest woman I ever met."

Why was my mother so angry? In 2017, getting serious about understanding my parents, I request my father's Harvard records—and they are a revelation.

# 2

# "Lazy and Lacking Ambition"

To send me my father's records and application for admission, Harvard wants a notarized photocopy of my passport, a copy of my father's death certificate, and the brief obituary the Waltham, Massachusetts, newspaper ran. I send them. And wait. And wait.

Several insistent letters later, the file arrives. My mother was positive that he was valedictorian of his high school class—not true. She thought he received all As, but his senior year report card is all Bs (English, Latin, German, Math, History). She thought he was Malden High class of 1936. Nope. He graduates in 1935, applies to Harvard—and Harvard turns him down.

Trained by my mother to be suspicious, I immediately wonder: Did my father feed her a line? Why did he think he could get into Harvard, with that unimpressive record? How did he eventually get in? Harvard records say he started out as a premed student, but his lack of interest in science—he could have taken a high school science course every year—and his C in Chemistry, the one science class he takes, suggest a lack of interest or aptitude.

I research further and realize that those B and C grades still allowed him to be ranked twentieth in a Malden High graduating class of 540: grade inflation has not yet set in. I see a notation that he attends Prozdor, an evening Hebrew high school for ten hours each week in Boston throughout his high school years, with classes (taught in Hebrew) in Bible, Talmud, contemporary Hebrew literature, and Jewish history.

Impressive, even though the "valedictorian" label is incorrect. Maybe my mother gradually came to believe that as part of her "brilliant but lazy" attack. But here's his typical Monday through Thursday: Malden High from 8:00 a.m. to 3:00 p.m. Jump onto the Boston Elevated Railway trolley (line 100 or 101) and head the ten miles to Prozdor in Boston's Roxbury neighborhood. Change trains at least once. Not easy—and more complications await.

Little Eli Olasky rarely encounters anti-Semitism. The Jewish residents of Malden total fifteen thousand, one-fourth of the city's total population. The Olasky home on 34 Upham Street is in the middle of Ward Seven, largely Jewish. In 1926 Eli is nine years old as he walks alongside his mother, Bertha, as she buys hallah and bagels from a Jewish baker. He looks in the eyes of fish on their beds of ice and unplucked chickens hanging by their wings on strings.

That's a little scary, but he looks up at his mother watching him. He feels secure as she buys kosher meat from a Jewish butcher, pickled herring and lox from a Jewish storekeeper. Outside, a man is playing a clarinet, and a few people throw pennies into a box. The tune is new, from a Jewish composer named George Gershwin. Bertha is improving her English and lilts a line from the song she has heard: "Someone to Watch over Me."

Now Eli is twelve, and his father, Louis, watches over him. They walk together to an Orthodox synagogue. He goes to the Young Men's Hebrew Association gym once a week and joins a junior Zionist literary club. Happily, his father is a coppersmith with a steady income used to pay off a loan for their three-story house, two floors of which he can rent out. Gamblers are losing money in the stock market, which crashes.

Eli goes to public school in the morning and Hebrew school in the afternoon. Many of his classmates also go to both. He is studious, serious, and quiet, so teachers in a large classroom appreciate him. He can lose himself in a book while the teacher tries to control the rambunctious.

Everything changes when he's fourteen and starts traveling back at night from Prozdor, the training ground for students who will go to Hebrew Teachers College (HTC). That's the profession his father wants him to follow. Prozdor and HTC are in a neighborhood of Boston not all that different from Malden: kosher butcher shops have sawdust on the floor and unplucked chickens heaped by the windows. But the area starting a few blocks away is dangerous terrain for Jews in the 1930s.

HTC student and future author Theodore White says roving gangs beat up Jewish teens. One of his *In Search of History* stories concerns a Jewish teen hurt by a gang on his trolley car. Later, he explains why he didn't get off: "I would have been killed." Journalist Nat Hentoff writes in his memoir, *Boston Boy*, "Some of the parochial school boys growlingly reminded us we were Jewish, and back in Roxbury, at night, it was still foolish to go out in the dark alone."

This is so different from my life—I never felt anti-Semitism—that I must dig deeper here. Dangerous times, the 1930s. Catholic priest Charles Coughlin is spewing hatred toward Jews on his national weekly radio show, the most popular in America. Boston Mayor James Michael Curley calls Boston "the strongest Coughlin city in the world." A few blocks from HTC, pro-Nazi meetings at Hibernian Hall attract as many as five hundred, with local leader Francis Moran leading a Heil Hitler salute. It's likely my father gets a beating at some point—but he never talks about it.

Other Boston area teens and their parents listen to the radio at night. WAAB has Buck Rogers episodes at 6:00 p.m. WEEI broadcasts *Amos 'n' Andy* at 7:00 p.m. and the Dorsey Brothers Orchestra at 8:00 p.m. WNAC has Guy Lombardo at 8:00 p.m. WBZ at 8:00 p.m. has *Fibber McGee and Molly.* My father goes to school and risks trolley travel.

That leads to questions: Why try for Harvard at all? Why not be a Hebrew school teacher, a white-collar professional, in America? It's a fine occupation for the son of an immigrant coppersmith from Ukraine who speaks little English. John Adams once listed the natural progression: he studies politics and war, his sons study history and commerce, their sons study painting and poetry. Louis Olasky: *I'm a coppersmith, Eli can become a Hebrew school teacher, my grandson can major in American Studies?*

A formal studio photo from 1932 suggests my grandfather's ambition for his sons: Eli and his younger brother David are dressed not like immigrant kids but as young gentlemen in suit coats with matching knickers, ties, and argyle knee socks. Most immigrant families put children to work after school to add to the family income. My grandparents emphasized education.

The one piece of my father's youthful writing I have suggests his own ambition. He declares in *The Stylus,* his school magazine, that Charles Dickens's books "seem to me like real, wide-awake persons with outstanding characteristics.

These literary acquaintances will never desert in time of trouble but will stand by me always." But if Roxbury toughs surround him, I suspect his literary acquaintances do not charge in to help.

Why Harvard? Its Widener Library has millions of books, which means millions of potential friends. My father's reading has opened up another world to him. Like most teenagers in the modern world, he wants to differentiate himself in some way from his father. Like many in this American land of opportunity, he has a way to do so. His father is a good man but still an uneducated peasant in many ways—or so an aspiring teen might view him. Eli Olasky can be an intellectual lord, if he gets into Harvard. One local history, *The Jews of Boston*, dubs acceptance to Harvard "a sacred rite of initiation of Jews, a sign that they had been accepted into the priesthood of the intellectual elite"—even "if they remained social outcasts as students, as many Harvard Jews did."

But what makes him think he can get in? Harvard in the 1930s has an informal quota for Jews of no more than 15 percent. That percentage rises to 25 percent in the 1924 freshman class, but A. Lawrence Lowell, Harvard's president from 1909 to 1933, says the presence of more Jews will lower the college's prestige and send its WASP core scurrying to Yale or Princeton.

Harvard does have one tenured Jewish professor: Harry Wolfson (1887–1974), a philosopher and historian with a chair in Hebrew literature created and paid for by a Jewish philanthropist. Wolfson is exceptional not only in his Harvard presence but also in his habits. One biographer, Isadore Twersky, portrays him "studying day and night, resisting presumptive attractions and distractions, honors and chores, with a tenacity which sometimes seemed awkward and antisocial."

Another biographer, Leo Schwarz, writes that even after Wolfson retires from the classroom, he is "still the first person to enter Widener Library in the morning and the last to leave it at night." My father would like to be like that.

President Lowell says he's not personally prejudiced, but he complains that 50 percent of students caught stealing books from Widener are Jewish. Then, asked how many students were caught, he confesses: two. Lowell says his only concern is that Harvard not become like Columbia University in this ditty of the era:

Oh, Harvard's run by millionaires,
And Yale is run by booze.
Cornell is run by farmers' sons,
Columbia's run by Jews.

Lowell says a college is like a fashionable resort hotel: No problem if a few Jews, the right kind, come—but if more come, WASPs will leave. Then Jews, social-climbing as they are in Lowell's stories, leave as well. Bankrupt hotel, dying Harvard. Such bigotry is too blatant for the Harvard faculty, which turns down Lowell's proposal for an official quota.

Harvard's admissions committee, though, quietly makes sure the percentage of Jewish students in the freshman class drops to 10 percent in 1930. The committee says some applicants' last names are not definitive, so it divides all "potentially Jewish" students into categories J1, J2, and J3, depending on the level of certainty about Jewishness.

I scrutinize my father's 1935 application. Questions about "father's occupation . . . country of origin . . . college attendance" are not idle curiosity. My father makes it easy for the admissions committee: Louis Olasky, coppersmith . . . Russia . . . no college." My father's recommendations include one from Mayer Slonim, his Hebrew teacher: "All the qualities which the rabbis of yore have enumerated in an exemplary student are found in him." A physician, S. Plohman, called Eli "a fine Hebrew scholar."

My father states his chief interest: Hebrew. He clearly knows nothing about ways to maximize his chances of getting in. But another of his recommenders, Abraham Smith, sees his drive: "He is industrious . . . and will keep on trying until he succeeds in his undertaking or the last vestige of hope is gone." So one turndown from Harvard doesn't destroy him. He still wants to get in—but how?

Enter Martin Nathanson, a Jewish graduate of Harvard who volunteers with a community organization, Boston Pace Associates. The charitable group creates mentoring relationships between college graduates and high potential high school students. Nathanson shows my father how to play the percentages and how to prepare a winning application. Nathanson writes to the admissions committee about his mentee, Eli Olasky: "I have been in a position to observe that he has qualities to make him a valuable addition to the student body of Harvard College."

What Nathanson knows, and my father does not, is that Harvard's admission system is rigged to make sure that, with rare exceptions, admitted students have not just the brains but the "character" to do well at Harvard. That means they should be gentlemen all, resolute but not pushy, well-spoken rather than talkative, triumphing without sweating.

Harvard admits in the 1930s more than 90 percent of applicants from leading prep schools like Phillips Exeter, Phillips Academy (Andover), St. Paul's, or Choate, but a tiny percentage from working-class schools like Malden High. My father was without the connections or the money to do prep school, but Nathanson tells him of a small third path: 75 percent of the applicants from Boston Latin, the city's elite public school, gain admission.

That knowledge does not at first seem useful. Eli has already graduated from high school. Boston Latin is only for Boston residents. But somehow, with Nathanson's help, he is able to attend Boston Latin for a "post-graduate" year. That willingness to help a few students from outside Boston may be part of Boston Latin's openness to Jewish students at a time when Harvard is still maintaining a cap: in 1936 half of Boston Latin's graduates are Jewish, yet (contra Lowell's predictions) non-Jews do not flee it.

Evenhandedness pays off for Boston Latin. When the school celebrates its 350th birthday in 1985 by publishing a piece about ten famous graduates, the first five are Cotton Mather, Benjamin Franklin, Samuel Adams, Ralph Waldo Emerson, and scientist Samuel Langley. The second five are Jewish: Nat Hentoff, Theodore White, Leonard Bernstein, art historian Bernard Berenson, and psychiatrist Robert Coles.

Boston Latin's policy also pays off for my father. He receives B grades during his year there, showing he can hang with Boston's best. Most important, his recommendations now come not from Jewish neighbors but from Boston Latin teachers and Headmaster Joseph Powers, who gives him As for personality, cooperation, and reliability of character, and calls him "a manly boy, mature, and likely to have very good influence on his fellows."

Regarding his interests, my father does not mention Hebrew. He lists astronomy, debating, tennis, and football. (I never see any interest in those when he's an adult.) The application works—just barely. In 1935 he passively waited for Harvard's acceptance or rejection. In 1936 he hounds the admissions office, writing on July 17, 1936, "I am sorry to inconvenience you at a time when you must be very occupied, but it is a matter of utmost importance to me."

Three days later he receives an admissions letter—but without any scholarship. That means he has to live at home, seven miles and an hour away from Harvard by streetcar and subway. He also has to come up with $400 a year for tuition, the equivalent of $7,400 now. The records show his father, who earns only $2,000 per year, cannot pay any of it. One contemporary writes that unless a student has at least $900 per year to spend at Harvard, it's best not to come. How does my father manage?

Trying to understand his experience, I seek out memoirs of Jewish commuting students in the late 1930s, like a real estate agent looking for "comps" of the houses they market. I find four: Robert A. Potash, Theodore White, Harry Katseff, and one anonymous student.

Robert A. Potash, author of *Looking Back at My First Eighty Years*, graduates from Boston Latin, obtains bachelor's and doctoral degrees from Harvard, then has an illustrious academic career as a Latin American history professor. He writes that his father wants him to have a Jewish education, so he studies for three years at Prozdor, "not too far from where we lived in Roxbury." For three years he studies Hebrew, Jewish history, and ceremonies. Then Dean Louis Hurwich invites him "to enroll in the Hebrew College itself" at the same time he attends Harvard.

Crucially, Potash refuses, and his parents back him up. Potash explains, "I was about to start my first year at college and I . . . felt that I could only undertake one time-consuming activity at a time. And since college was still an unknown world for me, I did not wish to jeopardize my prospects for success." His senior year math teacher, a Mr. Faxon, sends this recommendation to Harvard: "Potash has none of the characteristics usually ascribed to members of his race."

Potash not only gains acceptance but also receives a $300 per year scholarship. His father, who came to the United States in 1905 and is a fundraiser for Jewish organizations, evidently makes up the rest. The Potashes even move to Cambridge before Robert's junior year: the commute that was by streetcar and subway becomes one requiring only a walk.

My second top comp, Theodore White, graduates from both Boston Latin and HTC, receives a full $400 scholarship, commutes from home, graduates from Harvard in 1938, and goes on to write a famous series of books about presidential elections from 1960 through 1980. White writes in his autobiography that other students call commuters like himself (and my father) "meatballs: We were at Harvard not to enjoy the games, the girls, the burlesque shows, . . . the companionship, the elms, the turning leaves of fall, the grassy banks of the Charles. We had come to get a Harvard badge," a ticket to a good career.

White says commuters at lunchtime eat sandwiches from home and hang out in Harvard's drab Dudley Hall, where "intellectual upper-class communists" come to proselytize them for "the inevitable proletarian revolution." My father also brings a sandwich, but on days he feels rich he indulges: Ten cents for graham crackers, milk, and a bowl to slurp them in. Five cents for a chocolate bar that he eats between two slices of bread. Sometimes he pours free packets of ketchup into a bowl of hot water.

White says,

Most of us, largely Boston Latin School graduates, knew more about poverty than anyone from Beacon Hill or the fashionable East Side of New York. We hated poverty and meant to have no share of it. We had come to Harvard not to help the working classes, but to get out of the working classes. We were on the make . . . the approach to Harvard and its riches was that of a looter. Harvard had the key to the gates. What was behind the gates I could not guess, but all that lay there was to be looted.

White loots well, as do some other Dudley Hall students whom *Life* in 1941 labels "the untouchables." Journalist-historian David Halberstam says they had "none of the pleasures associated with young Harvard gentlemen. . . . Commuters were grinds. . . . They arrived, they studied, and they were whisked away by the MTA. It was as if they could be tolerated academically so long as they were not seen socially. Harvard to them was a classroom and a way station, little more, often more wounding than nourishing."

The two other comps I research are commuters and Boston Latin grads but not HTC students. Harry Katseff travels from Boston each morning and concentrates in chemistry, which means working in the chemistry lab until late afternoon. He then clerks in a cigar shop until midnight. He answers a question about his college life with a sigh: "What college life?" Katseff calls his Harvard time "a drab existence."

The fourth commuter, who speaks anonymously, earns spending money by tutoring wealthy students, but resents it: "I took notes for people, I even wrote term papers for all the rich kids who couldn't be bothered to go to classes. . . . Nobody ever invited me back to their rooms. [We were] second class citizens." Asked for good memories of Harvard, he says, "I got through, and that's what counts." A *Harvard Crimson* survey reveals bitterness among Dudley commuters, one of whom writes, "When people ask you what [residential] House you live in and you say you commute, their noses go up and their eyes cast 'that peasant' glances."

All four of the comps have to commute and work hard, but none has to jump five hurdles: twelve hours of classes at Harvard, thirteen at Hebrew Teachers College, ten hours of tutoring, twelve hours on streetcars and subways, and twenty-five hours of study time—a seventy-two-hour week. Eli Olasky's Harvard is not the Memorial Transept, with its black walnut paneling and sixty-foot-high gothic vault above a marble floor, with statues of Edmund Burke, Demosthenes, Cicero, William Pitt, and Daniel Webster.

The total number of black-tie Memorial dinners my father attends in what Henry James called "the great bristling brick Valhalla": zero. His Harvard is not that of tour books declaiming about imaginative stairway sequences, hammer-beam trusses, myriads of geometric patterns, and a John La Farge's *Athena Tying a Mourning Fillet* stained-glass window.

Occasionally my father climbs the stairs to Widener Library. James Engell, who becomes a Harvard professor of English, says the first time he ascends his legs are "literally trembling a little" as he thinks of all the treasures within. Engell says he always feels "more at home in Widener than any other place in the University" since the presence of millions of books encourages "slow concentrated thought."

That's something my father has little time for. His problem is not a lazy lack of ambition. He has a high DQ— determination quotient—to go alongside his high IQ. Besides, he's trapped. He could drop HTC, but through it he makes contacts to tutor adults in Hebrew. He needs the money, and he wants to avoid tutoring twelve-year-olds forced by their fathers to learn enough to avoid embarrassing themselves during lavish bar mitzvah observances.

As I research, I'm bonding with my father and thanking him as well. We were both in a hurry: he took two sets of classes at once, and I took an extra load to graduate in three years. But his road was much harder: I received a partial scholarship to Yale, lived on campus, and worked during the summer but not the school year. I could do that only because my parents paid $6,000 over those three years, the equivalent of $40,000 now.

And I returned kindness with scorn.

# 3

# One Shining Moment

Friday, November 20, 1936. Eli Olasky sits in the balcony of Harvard's biggest lecture hall. It has crimson walls. Large sets of windows line three of the walls—plenty of light. The seats rise gradually from a point seven feet in front of the platform to the rear of the room—plenty of visibility. They are made of oak, with a side desk that can be raised or lowered.

Steam heat raises the temperature to seventy-four degrees, and some students have been known to fall asleep. Not during this hour, though. On the stage Professor Earnest Albert Hooton imitates the posture and gait of an anthropoid ape, which he says is man's ancestor. He models a gibbon loping along, with raised arms grasping for a branch. The six hundred students, almost all wearing ties and tweed coats, laugh and applaud. So does my father, in a Filene's Basement sweater, although on this day he's just visiting, since he has a full schedule of chemistry and physics courses.

A student asks a question about the significance of heredity. Hooton tells a story about an anthropologist seeing a black-haired woman walking with a little boy who has flaming red hair. The anthropologist introduces himself and asks if she'll tell him the hair color of the boy's father.

"I don't know," the woman says. "He didn't take off his hat." The room erupts with laughter.

Hooton refers to a book he's written, *Apes, Men, and Morons*, and says, "In honor of all the stupid people, I will now recite a poem I have written, 'Ode to a Dental Hygienist.'" His last two lines are, "At least as far as she has gotten / She sees how much of me is rotten." He throws out more one-liners: "If marriages were made in a Ford factory rather than heaven, they'd last longer and be more efficient." At the end of the lecture, two students roll out a lavish cake as others sing, "Happy birthday to you." It's Hooton's forty-ninth.

Hooton is Harvard's most popular professor, one my father is eyeing as he tries to survive a miserable semester and to remember why he was excited about entering the university. Hooton will become nationally known, as *Life* in 1939 devotes six pages to Hooton and his lectures about the United States needing a "biological purge" of those intellectually and financially feeble. But right now my father needs a purge of his grades, because he's having two big problems.

One is time: multitasking at Harvard, HTC, tutoring, and commuting is hard. A second is the courses he's taking now that his father has raised his sights: his firstborn as a Hebrew teacher was a happy thought, but a doctor would even be better. And yet, my father is tiptoeing into trouble. A report from a physics professor shows him averaging 46 percent on biweekly tests and 56 percent on problem sets.

The spring term is even worse. An assistant dean writes on March 9, 1937, "The Administrative Board has voted to place you on probation because of your unsatisfactory record. . . . You are in serious danger of separation from the College at any time. . . . Readmission after an initial failure" is rare.

Somehow my father finds the time to study more. He barely passes all his spring semester classes. Premed courses engage neither his brain nor his heart. Rosalie Magruder, a secretary in Harvard College Dean A. C. Hanford's office, sends her boss a note: Eli Olasky was "pushed into a field in which he was not greatly interested by his father."

Somehow an intervention occurs. My grandfather realizes his son will not be a doctor. My father's faculty advisor and an assistant dean review a letter Louis Olasky sends. (Since he knew little English, I suspect my father was the ghostwriter.) The letter says Eli "confessed this to me about one of his Junior High School courses. It was Ancient History, in which he was interested. He read the text-book through as soon as he received it. His perusal was so thorough and comprehensive that he received high grades in the subject with but scanty reference to the text. His first reading and some notes that he had taken sufficed. This shows how far interest can carry him."

I picture Eli's faculty advisor giving him a hearty admonition: *Harvard isn't junior high school.* Harvard lets him change his intended major. But to what? Given my father's love of reading and Charles Dickens, an English major makes sense, but what will he do with it? University English departments are "an anti-Jewish stronghold," according to historian Lewis Feuer. Harvard's F. O. Matthiessen, author of *American Renaissance*, says "highly qualified Jews encounter difficulty . . . in finding more than an occasional appointment."

As my father considers majors, he continues his evening Hebrew Teachers College classes. HTC has none of Harvard's elegance. Classes are in rooms with scarred floors and mismatched furniture, but they are intellectually robust. Students sit in their coats, because heat is expensive. My father reads the Hebrew Bible in its original form—no vowel signs. He reads modern Hebrew literature and studies

Jewish history, with a few lectures on classroom management and teaching methods thrown in.

Historian Frank Manuel, who graduates from HTC in 1930, earns a Harvard PhD in 1933, and becomes a professor at Brandeis University when it opens in 1948, says, "I found Hebrew Teachers College more stimulating than Harvard." Some of the stimulation comes from HTC's dean, Samuel Perlman, who also edits the World Zionist Organization's Hebrew weekly, *Haolam*. He hires Zionist intellectuals who emphasize the uniqueness of Israel and teach "aesthetic nationalism," the romance of *tarbut*, Hebrew culture.

Other stimulation at HTC comes from studying the works of Yehezkel Kaufmann (1889–1963). He emphasizes faith in God as Judaism's unifying force and criticizes the then-dominant theories of Julius Wellhausen, who says the five books of Moses are not from Moses. Wellhausen postulates a discordant mix of four different texts, with influence from Canaanites and other practitioners of ANE (Ancient Near East) religions. Kaufmann, to the contrary, says monotheism was solely an Israelite development: "Israelite religion was an original creation of the people of Israel. It was absolutely different from anything the pagan world knew. Its monotheistic world view has no antecedents in paganism."

Also influential: Ben Halpern (1912–1990), who graduates from HTC and Harvard in 1932, joins Zionist groups, and during the 1940s edits the *Jewish Frontier*, a labor Zionist publication. He earns a Harvard PhD in sociology and gains his first professorial position, at Brandeis, when he is fifty. Halpern sees all Gentiles as inevitably anti-Semitic and stresses the importance of Jewish culture: His slogan for all Jews individually and collectively is *hagshama atzmit*, self-realization. He scorns those who "junk their scruples and standards in a single-minded scramble for promotion and power."

Harvard and HTC professors and students have different environments: elegant halls versus rooms that could use fresh paint. But many have something in common: scorn both for those who aren't as bright and for those who use their talent primarily in mercantile pursuits. One HTC slogan comes from the Talmud: "Thou shall not make of thy learning a spade wherewith to dig."

Once my father indicates a desire to concentrate in anthropology, Harvard assigns a lecturer in the field, Carleton Coon, to be his course advisor and occasional tutor. Coon, who came to Harvard from Phillips Academy (Andover) and graduated magna cum laude in 1925, argues that each race of *Homo sapiens* evolved separately from an earlier species, *Homo erectus*: "Each subspecies, living in its own territory, passed a critical threshold from a more brutal to a more *sapient* state."

My father and Coon early in September 1937 meet in Coon's small, stuffy office, with wall-to-wall bookcases and filing cabinets containing journals and artifacts. Coons says future evolution depends on eugenics both on an individual and a racial basis. So do many others. Princeton professor Edwin Conklin, president of the American Association for the Advancement of Science in 1936, explicitly calls whites more evolutionarily advanced than blacks. So does Columbia professor Henry Fairfield Osborn, president of the American Museum of Natural History's board of trustees.

This racism is common. Famed sportswriter Paul Gallico, reporting for the *New York Daily News* in 1935, asks about heavyweight boxer Joe Louis, "Is he all instinct, all animal? Or have a hundred million years left a fold upon his brain? I see in this colored man something so cold, so hard, so cruel that I wonder as to his bravery. Courage in the animal is desperation."

My father prefers Professor Hooton, who celebrates the sterilization in the United States of seventy thousand "imbeciles" but sees the racial question differently. He calls claims of "German racial purity" and supremacy baseless: "Joe Louis is probably as authentic an Aryan as [Hitler] and certainly an infinitely finer specimen of human being." Hooton doesn't hold with anti-Semitism either: he says Jews are intellectually superior because persecution over the centuries "eliminated their morons."

Coon, judging by his writing, would advise my father not to shy away from Charles Darwin's prediction in *The Descent of Man* that "the civilized races of man will almost certainly exterminate, and replace, the savage races throughout the world." Darwin placed blacks lower than whites on the line of civilization but higher than baboons. Coon says it's not the fault of the "inferior" people: Aryans and Chinese evolved two hundred thousand years earlier than Africans, so blacks in Coon's view are way behind.

Coon may have laid out explicitly the decision Harvard anthropology asks students to make. I'm not sure of the exact words, but the essence of Coon's question would be: *Will you live by "science," or something from thousands of years ago when people believed the sun could stand still?*

Soon it's the tenth day of Tishrei, 5698, according to the calendar hanging in the kitchen of 34 Upham Street. (My grandfather believed, and taught my father, that Adam and Eve lived in the garden of Eden in year 1, trusted their own logic rather than God's instruction, and then became the father and mother of all humanity.) But my father doesn't spend time in the kitchen on that tenth day because it is Yom Kippur, a fast day, the holiest day of the year, a time for all-day prayer to God, Creator of heaven, earth, and human life.

Two days later my father sits in an oak chair on the main floor of the large auditorium. Hooton directly challenges what Orthodox Jews believe. Anthropology A, according to Harvard's 1937 course catalogue, emphasizes the "physical origin of man, his evolution and man's place among the primates, racial criteria and classification." Physical anthropology is based on an evolutionary understanding of the biology of humans in relation to nonhuman primates and extinct hominid ancestors.

My father does well in Anthropology: Bs (genuinely above average grades in those days) as opposed to his pre-med Cs and Ds. In the fall of his junior year, Dean Hanford congratulates him for moving from Group VI among undergraduates, the lowest, to Group IV, with the prospect that "you will be able to make your standing still higher and get on the Dean's List."

My father hopes to graduate with honors and be one of the special twenty men admitted to Harvard's graduate school in anthropology—but it all depends on how professors receive his senior thesis. He has some qualms about the way professors are always classifying people by racial types, but they do see Jews as superior, so he thinks it's not dangerous. And, he can use part of what he's learned at HTC by writing about the culture of ancient Israel.

But as my father digs into the topic, he has to choose. Will he go with his childhood and HTC teaching that the Bible is a unique creation? Or will he run with the secular materialist view that the Israelites are just one more Ancient Near East tribe, with scriptures uninspired by God?

41

I realize I can obtain from Harvard a photocopy of my father's senior thesis. I'm eager to find out on which side he comes down on in 1940. When the package arrives from Cambridge, I rip it open and read my father's initial summary: "The civilization of the Israelites was a mixture comprising elements which they had brought in from the desert and elements which they had absorbed and assimilated after they had entered Canaan. Their nomadic inheritance had been common to all the Semitic nomadic peoples. From the common Semitic font in dim antiquity they drew their common source of knowledge, their social and religious institutions."

The thesis rolls on with solid specific detail about Israelite culture and practice. My father uses what he has learned at Hebrew Teachers College but abandons the underlying ethos. He writes that the Bible is "an interesting and excellent source of information, especially in regard to social life and custom." So is the *Encyclopaedia Britannica*. On page 213, the last page, he summarizes his conclusions concerning the supposedly God-breathed culture of ancient Israel: It grew out of "the traditions and culture which had spread all over Western Asia long before. In no way were the Israelites unique."

Louis and Bertha Olasky are filled with pride at the Harvard commencement on June 20, 1940. Carl Sandburg and Secretary of State Cordell Hull speak. The program is in Latin: page VII shows their Eli graduating *CVM LAVDE*, with honors. Some of the names are strange, like Christianvs Marivs. But right above Georgivs Robertvs and Georgivs Washington Osgood is plain Eli Olasky.

That is a remarkable achievement for someone almost kicked out as a freshman. Louis Olasky buys five copies of the *Boston Globe*, which lists all the graduates in English. On the front page, though, is news of the German army routing the French. General Charles de Gaulle broadcasts over the BBC: "It is the duty of all Frenchmen who still bear arms to continue the struggle." On June 22, France surrenders to Germany.

Having adjusted his views to conform to Harvard anthropology, my father on August 8, 1940, receives this letter: "I am happy to inform you that you will be admitted to this school. . . . On the day following registration you should consult Professor E. A. Hooton, Chairman of the Department of Anthropology, and formulate a program for the Master's degree that meets with his approval."

One month later they meet in Hooton's office. It's unlike Coon's or any other Harvard office my father has visited. Shelves along one wall hold dozens of skulls. Other shelves have collections of human teeth: orthodontists once a year come to hear Hooton talk about the evolution of bicuspids and molars. I suspect the discussion goes like this: Hooton asks my father which undergraduate anthropology courses he liked the most. He thinks for a moment and responds, *Races and cultures—Africa, Oceana, Europe, and aboriginal America. I suppose I like the storytelling aspects.*

That's fine, Hooton replies, but to get a master's degree students must learn the basics of research. Eli Olasky must learn how to measure heads, noses, and buttocks to see racial distinctives and to see how humans relate to our fellow primates, such as baboons. He will spend hours each week in a basement room at a large table piled high with pottery pieces of different colors, markings, and shapes. He will learn the who, what, when, and where of each shard. But it won't be all work, Hooton assures my father: he will be expected at afternoon teas in the Hooton house, where he can fill up with jasmine tea and Scottish shortbread.

My father says he's not much of a partygoer. "Nonsense," Hooton replies. His goal is to save humanity from the deterioration that is inevitable unless nations embrace eugenic principles. He needs graduate students willing to set up physical anthropology programs in every university. Hooton also knows that every university has its academic politics, and social graces are as important as intellectual rigor. The afternoon tea is training in intellectual repartee. Besides, Hooton says, "You people are good at arguing." Bigotry killed off the weaker Jews, and what's left are mighty warriors.

I research the careers of some Hooton tea party attenders. Richard B. Woodbury, born like my father in 1917, attains a Harvard MA in 1942 and a PhD in 1948. His dissertation is "Prehistoric Stone Implements of Northeastern Arizona: A Study of the Origin, Distribution, and Function of the Stone Tools, Ornaments, and Weapons of the Jeddito District." Woodbury specializes in southwestern archaeology and founds the anthropology department at the University of Massachusetts—fulfilling Hooton's hopes.

Another success, Sherwood Larned Washburn, grows up in Cambridge and is an unpaid volunteer at the Museum of Comparative Zoology while in prep school. Biographer David Browman says Washburn "faithfully attended the tea Earnest Hooton gave every afternoon at his home, which all graduate students attend." Washburn specializes in what we can learn about humans by studying our relatives among the primates; his dissertation is titled "A Preliminary Metrical Study of the Skeletons of Langurs and Macaques." Washburn becomes chairman of the University of Chicago anthropology department. Mission accomplished.

Others have odder successes. Paul Gebhard born in 1917, gains his undergraduate degree in 1940, just like my father. He receives his PhD after defending a dissertation on "Stone Objects from Prehistoric North America with Respect to Distribution, Type, and Significance." Gebhard joins Alfred Kinsey at Indiana University, dives into sexual research, and in 1956 becomes the Kinsey Institute's second director. Gebhard retires in 1982 at age sixty-five and lives for another thirty-three years as the United States' premier sexologist.

My father is not a success in graduate school. He has his Bachelor of Jewish Education diploma from HTC and now has more time, but he lacks small talk and never laughs—this is apparently a lifetime characteristic, at least as an adult. He does not show well at Hooton's teas. The work of physical anthropology is not as interesting as the undergraduate classes in cultural anthropology: Columbia's anthropology department emphasizes cultural aspects rather than the shape of heads, and he would have been better off there.

A philosophical concern comes to the fore early in 1941 when a Jewish professor at Columbia, Bernhard J. Stern, attacks Hooton's "anti-democratic, ruthless, social-Darwinian utterances." He says, "Hooton has become the scientific playboy of fascist and neofascist groups." That's an over-the-top assault, but Hooton was on the advisory council of what became the American Eugenics Society.

It's hard not to ask questions. Hooton likes Jews and "only" wants to sterilize the mentally incompetent of every ethnic group—but is treating some humans as subhuman only a mutation away from the developing horror stories in Germany and Poland? It's one thing to write abstractions in academic journals, but my father has vulnerable relatives in Hitler's path.

My father's interest in cultural anthropology rather than physical anthropology makes him academically incorrect in

Hooton's graduate program. His awkwardness at afternoon teas makes him socially incorrect. The third strike comes when he wonders whether the thinking behind Hooton's eugenics is a second cousin—maybe even a first—to Nazi policies.

# 4

# Seeing the Worst

On a warm day in July 1941, my father at 4:00 p.m. is sitting not at a Hooton tea but with his father as they drink hot tea in glasses with metal cupholders, Russian style. My grandfather puts a cube of sugar between his teeth and sips the tea through it. My father drinks it straight. They are reading *The Forward*, the Yiddish newspaper with a national circulation of 175,000. It's three weeks since Germany went to war against Russia, putting their relatives in the Ukraine in jeopardy as Hitler's troops drive eastward.

My grandmother puts in front of my father an envelope that has just arrived with a Harvard University return address. I'm looking at a copy of the letter, dated July 10, from graduate school associate dean L. S. Mayo. He writes, "I am hoping you have not set your heart on returning to this school in September—because something stands in your way, and it devolves on me to tell you so." Mayo says anthropology professors have decided my father "cannot profit sufficiently by further graduate work to make it advisable" for him to continue at Harvard: "We shall not expect you to register in the fall."

The file I receive from Harvard graduate school does

not include my father's graduate school grades. Repeated requests yield neither a transcript nor any warning letters. My surmise: Mayo's eviction notice comes as a lightning bolt from Olympus. I suspect my father groans and walks to his room. Later, he tells his parents. Louis says the *goyim* (non-Jews) have done him wrong. My father says it's more complicated than that.

My father never talks about his expulsion from anthropology, but I suspect it must have come hard. He went all out in his senior thesis to become a Harvard man. A Hooton man. Now Hooton and associates say he isn't worthy. My father has doubts about Hooton's philosophy. Shard-studying classes and Scottish shortbread are not my father's cup of tea—but it's hard to be kicked out, especially when only several courses short of a master's degree.

Eli Olasky, HTC and Harvard graduate, could teach in Malden Hebrew School, but his ambitions have grown. He sits at home for several weeks, psychologically paralyzed. His mother dotes on him. His father continues going to work every day at the Atlantic Works in East Boston. Incorporated in 1853, Atlantic Works specializes in the building of engines and boilers. It boasts fourteen acres of modern machinery, now equipped with floodlights—because if war comes, the facilities will be used around the clock.

Louis Olasky tells my father, *Komm mit mir.* They take the streetcar and subway to Maverick Square, a five-minute walk from the Atlantic Works. Louis shows him the powerhouse. Four hundred 40-volt motors. Two 100-horsepower Scotch dryback boilers. A motor-driven 1,600 cubic foot capacity air compressor, with a steam-driven one on standby. A fifteen-ton crane. A two-hundred-ton hydraulic wheel press. It's manly work, with radial drills, horizontal and vertical boring mills, slotters and shapers, lathes of various sizes, and hydraulic pipe benders, grinders and drills.

I don't know how that father-son show-and-tell works, but I suspect foreman Louis says: *We're hiring, it's steady work, I can get you in.* My father agrees to work alongside his father for a while, until he figures out what to do.

After the Japanese bomb Pearl Harbor on December 7, 1941, many Americans enlist to fight on land or on sea, and others face a draft. Louis, now in charge of making boilers for submarines, certifies that his son works in an essential war industry. My father works all day, reads in the evening, and eats his mother's meals. He can sit out the war at home and in the factory, reading without the previous eight years of rushing.

A year later father and son return from work and sit at the kitchen table. I can visualize my grandmother bringing them plates of chicken and an opened envelope with a letter. Her eyes are red from weeping. The letter recounts events in Olevsk and Korets, the Ukrainian towns in which she and Louis spent their childhoods. Three men who survived— Tevel Trosman, Iakov Shklover, and Aleksei Makarchuk— tell how Ukrainians made three hundred Olevsk Jews tear out grass with their teeth, and what happened next.

I dig out those reports and learn that German troops march five hundred to nine hundred Jewish men, women, and children to a ravine two miles from Olevsk. The soldiers force them to remove all their clothes and stand in front of pre-dug trenches. The Germans shoot, and Jews drop. Each group falls onto the bodies of previous victims. The parents of Louis, Eli's grandparents, may have been among the victims.

The news from Korets is also horrible. Yitzhak Feiner, left for dead by the Germans, sneaks away at night and tells how Germans on May 21, 1942, took "men and women, six at a time, and led them to a pit, after each had to undress and remain naked. In the pit they were made to lie face down and on the edge of the pit six Germans, ready with their revolvers, shot the six victims in the head."

Feiner's account in Yiddish relates how German soldiers before shooting pull out of a pit Yakov Hirschenhorn, a doctor who has patched up some of them. They tell him to go home: "He begged to let his wife go with him, but the murderers did not agree. He went back into the pit and was shot with the others."

Feiner also describes German soldiers seizing Jewish children and throwing them into "horse-driven wagons just like one would throw stones. The murderer would seize the child—by the little hand, by the leg, by the head or by the shirt—and throw it into the wagon. The wagons were loaded full with the children, one on top of the other, [who] were thrown, alive, straight from the wagon into a pit. After two wagons were unloaded this way, two grenades were thrown in, tearing the children apart."

I can picture Louis folding the letter, standing up, putting on his *tallis*—his blue and white fringed shawl—and swaying as he prays. My father reacts with less prayer, more anger. Maybe his thoughts parallel those of screenwriter Ben Hecht, who says, "I felt only a violence toward the German killers. I saw the Germans as murderers with red hands." Many years later, in 2013, I feel a bit of that when I visit Olevsk and retrace the two miles to death some of my relatives walked.

In January 1943 my father is in the audience at pillared Temple Kehillath Israel in Brookline. The speaker is Max Weinreich, a refugee from Hitler's Europe. Kehillath Israel's four-columned limestone façade is imposing, but Weinreich's goal is to break up facades by "confessing publicly to a sense of burning shame for living in peace in this blessed land, in security and in plenty, at a time when the murderers' long knives have already butchered so many of our brothers and sisters across the sea."

From the depths of woe, Weinreich laments. He describes a report to President Franklin Roosevelt that says the Nazis have murdered two million Jews at that point. It decries Hitler's "edict calling for the total extermination of the over five million Jews who may still be alive in Nazi-dominated Europe." Weinreich is one of 283 scholars who sign a petition addressed to Roosevelt. It proposes that the United States should "apply hitherto unused methods" to save the additional five million threatened Jews. It is not specific about those methods.

Weinreich is forty-eight. Most of the 283 scholars are older. Eli Olasky is only twenty-five. He can apply one "hitherto unused method": enlist. He wants to be in on the fight against Hitler, even if it means huge personal adjustments. He gives up his deferment, enters the Army Air Corps on March 17, 1943, and goes to basic training in Florida.

Army life is hard. No privacy. Rude people. Little time to read. Meals of pork almost every day. Day after day my father does what he does not enjoy, but he gains approval as a marksman and a parachute rigger who can also handle armaments and other supplies. He heads to England on the *Louis Pasteur* on March 14, 1944. He disembarks at Liverpool on March 22, some thirty years and eleven months after his father had left there.

My father packs parachutes to support the D-Day drops of soldiers into Normandy. He doesn't see soldiers in his own unit die until September 2, when three of them are loading land mines onto a C-47. A sack falls off a truck and lands hard onto bundles of mines. They blow up. The explosion leaves a crater: Staff Sergeant Irving Brezack writes that in the crater "all we saw was someone's dog tag and an open pocket Bible." Medics dig one hundred sixty-five pieces of shrapnel out of the body of crew chief Roland Dahlberg, who is standing in the doorway of a plane when the bundle blows up. Dahlberg survives.

The army records I obtain show my father in a support capacity in England, then Italy, then France. When Germany surrenders in May 1945, his army group's activity, according to an official history, "increased rather than lessened by war's ending." The reason: "Now there were hundreds of thousands of liberated prisoners and displaced persons to be rushed homeward. Emergency food and medical cargoes had to be rushed to critical areas throughout Europe, wherever hunger or disease threatened."

The Air Force Historical Research Agency says my father's unit, during the months after World War II in Europe ended, transported displaced persons, many of whom were concentration camp survivors. Looking for detailed records on my father's squad, I file a federal form SF-180, "request pertaining to military records." The sad response: They burned up in a fire at a St. Louis warehouse two decades ago. No copies exist. So while I know his army group took care of concentration camp survivors, I don't know exactly where he went.

Here's what almost certainly happened, since the army when not fighting has a way of putting empty hands to work. Growing up in a Yiddish-speaking household and receiving high honors in German, Eli is a logical choice to help out at German concentration camps a short distance from where he is stationed.

He probably sees at such camps survivors staggering among piles of dead bodies, mutilated and emaciated. German guards didn't have time to burn or bury all their victims. He probably sees the floors of huge cremation ovens piled high with bone ash. Some camps have thousands of corpses stacked like logs waiting for the fireplace—logs with skeletal faces. Limbs dangle from naked gray trunks. Some small buildings contain formaldehyde jars of hearts, fingers, and eyes.

He probably goes to Buchenwald, about five miles from Weimar, Germany. Here's how Edward R. Murrow on CBS Radio reported his visit to a barracks there: "1,200 men in it, five to a bunk. The stink was beyond all description. . . . As we walked out into the courtyard, a man fell dead. Two others, they must have been over 60, were crawling toward the latrine. I saw it, but will not describe it."

What long-term effect did seeing such horror have on my father? Hard for me to know, since he never talked about this, but another soldier, Harry Herder, remembered how Buchenwald affected him: "Over fifty years ago, I went through a set of experiences that I have never been able to shake from my mind. They subside in my mind, and, then, in the spring always, some small trigger will set them off and I will be immersed in these experiences once more."

Herder adds, "There is no gradual diminution with time. . . . This year I set those memories on paper, all of them, or at least all of them I recall. I hope for the catharsis. I do not expect a complete purging—that would be expecting too much—but if I can get these memories to crawl deeper into my mind, to reappear less vividly, and less frequently, it will be a help."

I don't know exactly what my father saw and experienced, but something changed him from an ambitious young man interested in scholarly research to a stoic who tried to escape into science fiction and mystery dime novels. Part of it may have been what today we call PTSD, post-traumatic stress disorder. The horror may also have moved his career thinking from anthropology, where he wasn't welcome anyway, to the preservation of Jewish culture.

The post-war story was not "1.25 million Jews survive and live happily ever after." My father may be one of the soldiers who, during the summer of 1945, guide fact-finder Earl Harrison as he tours camps for "displaced persons" (DPs) in southern Germany. Harrison tells President Harry S. Truman that the United States in those camps is "treating the Jews as the Nazis treated them except that we do not exterminate them. They are in concentration camps in large numbers under our military guard instead of S.S. troops. One is led to wonder whether the German people, seeing this, are not supposing that we are following or at least condoning Nazi policy."

Harrison gives specific detail. One camp has no kitchen, another has starvation-level food supplies, and in many centers the DPs still wear their striped concentration camp uniforms. Latrine facilities are decrepit. Germans are getting their homes back, but Jews are still behind barbed wire: one 1,600-square-foot building at Bergen-Belsen houses eighty-five people.

Part of the horror Harrison and my father see reflects the extreme poverty of battered Europe: not much food generally. Part is politics: Hundreds of thousands of the Jewish DPs want to go to Palestine, and the British who still control that land are trying to placate Arab forces by holding the number to two thousand per month.

Eugenic bigotry also plays a part: Earnest Hooton saw Jews as above-average intellectually, but General George S.

Patton sees them as "locusts . . . a subhuman species without any of the cultural or social refinements of our times." When a United Nations aid distributor says concentration camp life has traumatized Jewish DPs, Patton responds, "I doubt it. I have never looked at a group of people who seem to be more lacking in intelligence."

The typical response to Holocaust revelations among Jews in 1945 is: Don't let Hitler win! I'm not sure how many children are conceived with that thought in mind, as well as other thoughts, but many Jewish post-war conferences have titles like "The Rebuilding of Jewish Life." When my father returns to the Boston area early in December, after his honorable discharge from the army, he visits Hebrew Teachers College, thinks about becoming part of that rebuilding, and learns about the latest provocation by a conservative rabbi turned radical theologian, Mordecai Kaplan.

Kaplan has just published a new prayer book that angers Orthodox rabbis: A group of them burn a copy inside New York's Hotel McAlpin on the corner of Broadway and Thirty-Fourth Street. (The largest hotel in the world when built in 1912, it becomes an apartment building that I live in for six months in 2007.) The Orthodox response, coming only a few years after Nazi burning of Jewish books, makes the *New York Times* and newspapers across the country.

Kaplan's prayer book omits references to basic Jewish doctrines. God punishes evil? Gone. Jews as the chosen people? Gone. A supernatural God who hears prayers? Gone. It's not clear why Jews with that worldview need a prayer book, but Kaplan calls it an aid to contemplation that will reach the hearts of young, skeptical Jews: Otherwise, Kaplan writes, "The motions survive; the emotions have fled. The lips move, but the heart is unmoved."

The Union of Orthodox Rabbis of the United States

and Canada calls Kaplan a heretic and decides "to excommunicate him and to separate him from the community of Israel until he fully repents. . . . The curse of the rabbis that has no remedy is upon anyone who holds this *siddur* in his hand or who looks at it, whether in private or in public." This is theological war. When Kaplan's youngest daughter tries to buy Sabbath cakes and bread from a local kosher baker, he refuses to serve her. Kaplan writes in his diary, "We have rabbinical gangsters who resort to Nazi methods in order to regain their authority."

My father buys a copy of Kaplan's major work, *Judaism as a Civilization*. It's probably the same copy I see in his bookcase many years later and eventually read. In it Kaplan praises Judaism as a result of natural human development rather than divine inspiration. He says the Hebrew Bible is not God's Word, but merely a key document in the evolving religious civilization of the Jewish people. He says Noah's flood was not a mega-drowning but a writer's device to get our attention. He says the book of Exodus is a work of fiction rather than an actual history of liberation from bondage.

Kaplan says children and college students are abandoning Judaism and should learn that biblical accounts of "creation, the flood, the Patriarchs, Moses, the exodus [are] ancient religious folklore." Such instruction will end "mental conflict which has alienated Jewish youth from their religion." For the sake of the children, "it is necessary frankly to recognize as products of the popular imagination all those elements in [the Bible] that cannot be maintained as actual or historic fact."

Kaplan says the thinking of education reformer John Dewey and sociologist Émile Durkheim makes it foolish for Jews to maintain Judaism's traditional theological claims. Kaplan says, "The objective study of history has established the fact that the records of miracles are unreliable, and that the stories about them are merely the product of the popular imagination." Surprisingly, he announces this as good news: "Beliefs similar to those found in the Bible about God arise among all people at a certain stage of mental and social development." That's what my father wrote in his senior thesis.

Kaplan declares, "The people of Israel began its life as did every other nation." That means every other nation can accomplish what Israel has. He says, "The truths established by the various sciences of human nature and history no longer permit us to concede that Israel received a type of revelation or communication that was outside the order of nature." That means all people can naturally ascend. The theory of evolution is not only true but joyful: "The Darwinian conception of the descent of man from the lower animals . . . holds forth the promise of man's evolving into a much higher type of being than he is now."

Kaplan also publishes a new prayer book for Passover meals that minimizes the miracles of the Exodus story and eliminates references to God condemning the enemies of the Jewish people. That may not seem like a big deal now, since a trip to Amazon yields titles like *Haggadah for Jews and Buddhists*, *A Hip-Hop Haggadah*, *The Hyper-Modern Ancient With-It Traditional Haggadah*, the *Love and Justice Haggadah* (for LGBT users), and the punny *Haggadah Good Feeling about This*. But it's a big deal then, because Orthodox rabbis see Kaplan ripping out the heart of their observances.

My father's reaction is different: Kaplan helps him meld his Harvard studies and part of HTC's teaching. Judaism has no objective validity as a religion, because it does not come from God. As a civilization, though, it is subjectively valuable, because it gives Jews a place in the world and a common bond. The Nazis wanted to make Jews extinct.

Continued anti-Semitic pressures make Jews an endangered species. But Jews should hold on, because if Judaism disappears their distinct contribution to human society vanishes.

Kaplan says he will hold on despite criticism: His supporters should not give up the field of Jewish education to the Orthodox. And my father should hold on. Maybe Judaism, understood this way, is like a Disney story—but *It's our Disney story.* Yes, that turns Judaism into a club—but a club worth continuing. My father has hit upon a practical theology that he will hold to for the rest of his life: a courageous although self-contradictory desire to preserve Judaism without preserving the essence of Judaism, the belief in a personal God who is not only transcendent but immanent.

As 1946 begins he thinks about whether to make use of his graduate school credits. He has been kicked out of the Anthropology program but is eligible to apply for readmission to Harvard Graduate School in a different department, if one will accept him. The GI Bill will pay his tuition, and Harvard is reluctant both to turn down money and to frustrate a veteran. Getting a master's degree won't necessarily help him in the world of Hebrew school teaching but it's an impressive credential.

# 5

# Someone to Watch over Me

On January 22, 1946, my father sits on the other side of an oak desk the size of an aircraft carrier. He's in the office of Payson S. Wild, Jr., the dean of Harvard Graduate School. I suspect Wild exudes sympathy for an obviously distressed veteran kicked out of the anthropology department four and a half years earlier.

"Harvard wants to give veterans every opportunity to continue their education," Wild intones. "Anthropology, though, has shut the door on you. What do you think would suit you more?" My father is silent. Wild gives his face some hard scrutiny: "What about Semitic languages and history?"

Later, Wild scribbles a note: "Olasky says he wants to change fields, possibly to Semitics." It's a small program that's a refuge for a few Jewish students. Wild continues: "Seems to be vague and looked through the catalogue at random. Told to get clearance and advice from both Tozzer and Pfeiffer. Will need letter from Anthropology and the new department of his choice (if any) in order to gain read-mission."

Key words: "If any." Does Eli Olasky really want to be an academic? Before the war, my father is on fire with ambition. He knows the regulations. Now he's "vague."

Two weeks later he has an appointment with Alfred Marston Tozzer, now chairman of the anthropology department. Tozzer, sixty-eight, has a smaller desk, but walls exhibit career highlights. A plaque commemorates his exhibition in 1921 at the Second International Congress of Eugenics. On a shelf sits a Mayan totem that he brought back from Yucatán in his suitcase.

Tozzer welcomes my father, soldier to soldier. Tozzer has just returned from a two-year assignment as director of the Honolulu office of the Office of Strategic Services (predecessor of the CIA). One reason he asks for and receives that assignment is that he and his wife for years summered on Oahu. While there he measured and compared the bodies of Chinese Hawaiians and their white Hawaiian neighbors.

Tozzer's secretary buzzes him: The *Harvard Crimson* is profiling him and he needs to respond to a fact-checking call. While he's out, my father looks at a framed copy of a *Boston Globe* article on the wall. It's from 1936, when Tozzer chairs Harvard's Tercentenary Committee.

The two hundredth anniversary was celebrated on September 8, 1836, but Tozzer's committee settled on September 18, 1936, because in 1636 the colonists used a Julian calendar: September 18 makes for an exact three hundred years, given the introduction of the Gregorian calendar. Jewish alumni protest, since September 18 is also the date of Rosh Hashanah, the Jewish New Year's Day when many have synagogue obligations. Tozzer held firm.

Tozzer returns and says he's glad to write a letter passing on my father to the Semitics department. I scrutinize a copy of that letter, dated February 6. Tozzer tells Dean Wild, "Olaskey [sic] asked me to relieve him from our report that he was unacceptable. . . . I have no desire to prevent Mr. Olaskey from going into Semitics, even if we are not enthusiastic about him ourselves." On March 14, Robert Pfeiffer, who chairs Semitic Languages and History, gives his assent. Eli Olasky can start in the fall.

In April the weather turns warm. Eli Olasky, twenty-eight, sits two blocks from his parents' home in a park still with its colonial name, Ferryway Green. It has tennis courts: he may be playing, or reading with his back against a tree. A pretty twenty-seven-year-old, Ida Green, walks over to him. Years later she tells me, "He wasn't handsome, but he was good-looking." The war is over. For both of them, it's time to settle down.

Eli takes Ida for ice cream at the Shan-Lor Drugstore on Cross Street. Shan-Lor has a juke box that's playing a cut from *The Voice of Frank Sinatra*, the first studio album by the young singer: "Someone to Watch over Me." The prime song's refrain: "Won't you tell her please to put on some speed / Follow my lead. . ." The album has gone to number one on the just-started Billboard album chart.

Eli doesn't talk much, so Ida tells him about her family. Both her parents were immigrants early in the century, like his. Her father works very hard and has built his own business, United Bedding. Two of her brothers and one of her sisters work for him, as does a brother-in-law. Her mother is sick—but she doesn't give details, and my father does not ask many questions.

She asks him about Harvard, which she thinks must be a magical place, like the palaces depicted in the Texaco Metropolitan Opera broadcasts she listens to on the radio on Saturday afternoon. He's impressed that she listens to operas. He's never had time to listen to music, or much interest in it beyond Gilbert and Sullivan. He doesn't want to talk about Harvard.

They seem on first glance to be much alike. They grew up within a mile of each other and probably brushed by in the corridors of Malden High, although he was on the college track a year ahead of her and she was on the business track. They're both Jewish, although she has almost never gone to synagogue and knows little about Judaism. She never went to college, but she seems smart enough.

Another week goes by. A refugee teacher at Malden Hebrew School falls ill, so my father agrees to fill in as he waits to begin his Semitic studies at Harvard. Eli and Ida have their next date on Saturday evening. They meet in Malden's Suffolk Square. She talks about her favorite places there: the 5&10, the movie theatre, and particularly Berman's Dry Goods, packed with clothing and fabrics: "Don't you like the way they hang dresses and suits from the ceiling and bring them down with that long, hooked stick?" My father says, "I never noticed."

Berman's has a radio tuned at 8:00 p.m. to WEEI and the Dorsey Brothers Orchestra. Frank Sinatra is singing a 1940 song by Johnny Mercer: "Fools Rush In (Where Angels Fear to Tread)."

I suspect that my mother, while being charming as she could be, would still let my father know some of her frustrations: how she has to hand her father most of her secretary's paycheck—food, plus rent for a bed at home that she finally has to herself now that four of her brothers and sisters are married. She tells him she remembers coming to the market there with her mother, who fished in barrels for garlic pickles, or bobbed her kerchiefed head to pluck from a low shelf a tray of chopped liver or a carton of eggs.

She waits for him to tell her something about his memories, but he remains quiet, so, seeking understanding, she says more: "My parents fight about food at times. He says, 'I want a *berryer* [a woman with good domestic skills], but you give me *chazerei* [garbage], and worse than *chazerei—dreck.*'" My mother giggles: "She calls him a *fershtinker.*"

My father doesn't laugh, but he's paying attention to her, which few people do. She yearns for a husband with a high IQ but also a high EQ—emotional quotient—and she convinces herself that he can be the one.

The courtship moves fast. Eli and Ida meet again at Ferryway Green. He and his parents live only two blocks away, and he invites her to meet them. They walk slightly uphill. Then they're inside at 34 Upham Street, in his parents' living room. Stuffed chairs topped with antimacassars, small cloths to prevent soiling of the fabric. A tombstone-like cabinet for a radio and record player, with a walnut veneer. On a side table: a piece of sheet music, "Leben zol Amerika" (Long Live America), with pictures of George Washington, Abraham Lincoln, and the Statue of Liberty.

Ida reads the lyrics as Eli summons his parents from their screened-in porch. The song begins, "To express loyalty with every fiber of one's being, to this Land of Freedom, is the sacred duty of every Jew." She gets no further, because her future parents-in-law walk in. I have no idea what they talk about, and my mother's Yiddish by then is rusty—but they smile a lot, and Louis has his arm around Bertha.

My grandparents retreat to their porch. My mother says, "Your parents like each other." My father replies, "Of course they do. They're married." My mother begins a sentence—"But what happens when . . ." Then she decides Eli doesn't know her well enough to go down that path.

The next step is meeting Ida's father, Robert Green. Since this is America, Eli and Ida do not require his consent, but good manners and good finances demand a visit. It's nine years since *Snow White* played in the Suffolk Square movie house, and my mother came out of the theater singing, "Someday My Prince Will Come." She's now past that romanticism, but she would still like a memorable wedding at Chateau Guirard in Brookline—which her tight-fisted father will have to pay for.

At 8:00 p.m. Eli Olasky sits at Robert Green's kitchen table. My father planned to arrive after dinner, but his future father-in-law works late and is now tearing into the flesh of a boiled chicken and sucking its toes. He also eats a little whitefish, stripping the meat with his teeth and sucking on the head.

Dinner consumed, Robert Green asks some questions in Yiddish: *What's your monthly income?* He's not pleased with the answer. *So what did you gain by going to your fancy college?* No satisfactory answer there. He takes a drink from his Coke glass, half full of whiskey and rum.

Robert Green shows my father a 9" x 12" photograph of a wedding the previous year he has just finished paying for. I have that photo, or a copy of it. The star of that show, Bessie, my mother's older sister, is standing in the middle of the front row next to the tall husband she has just married. He's in his US Navy sailor's suit. Bessie's married sisters sit in front holding corsages. Their husbands stand behind them. Robert Green is prominent in a tuxedo and a top hat, smirking in apparent enjoyment of a dress-up joke.

Way at the back, standing alone, is an unsmiling, sad-eyed woman, my mother. Robert Green points to her and says, in Yiddish, she's been a good girl, earning money for the family during the ten years since her high school graduation. He puffs on his Lucky Strike and says *zi fardint es*, she deserves it. He'll pay for the wedding. But he says Bessie's husband, Al, has started a junkyard and will become rich. What will Eli do? Go to more classes at that Harvard? How does that put bread on the table?

My grandfather smokes that cigarette down to a tiny butt, holding it with his yellow fingernails. He then removes the remaining scrap of paper so he can save the remnant of tobacco for smoking in his pipe. He calls his pet cat over to his chair, holding up the small fish skeleton. When the cat comes closer, he kicks it and offers Eli advice: *If Ida gets out of line, belt her. And if you have children and they get out of line, use your belt on them.*

So, maybe only a month after they first met, the plans are made: August 20, 1946, at the Chateau. It's a splendid affair. I stare at a photo of my father in a tuxedo and my mother in a long white gown. I can only speculate about what's going on in their heads. They each now have someone to watch over them, but their goals are different. She tells him she never had a doll to play with, a birthday present to enjoy, or a college course to attend. She just wants the basics.

Seven years before, Ida Green's first trip away from home was by train to New York City. She visited the 1939 World's Fair and peeked at the Metropolitan Opera stage. Back in Malden, before coming home, she stopped in Suffolk Square and bought flowers for her mother. When she presented them, her mother replied, "I don't care"—and went to bed, turning her face to the wall.

On August 20, 1946, I suspect my mother is delighted. She and her new husband are wearing elegant clothes. Think of Texaco Metropolitan Opera announcer Milton Cross announcing the wedding to his twelve million listeners on Saturday afternoon: "The curtains are parting now. Eli and Ida Olasky are taking their bows. Listen to the cheers and applause. This will go on and on."

Her favorite opera is *Turandot*. The climax comes when the Prince of Tartary sings the harrowing aria, "Nessun Dorma," with its top-of-the-lungs one-word culmination: "Vincerò," which translates as *I will win*. She's marrying a Harvard graduate. VINCERÒ.

My father's thoughts may have been more complicated. In two weeks, he's supposed to start graduate school in Semitic languages and history. His senior thesis is coming back to haunt him. Since he agrees that the Bible was derived from other ANE (Ancient Near East) religions, he has to be able to read those documents, although he's not particularly interested in spending his time that way. In particular, he has to spend his first year learning ancient Assyrian, Syriac, and Arabic.

Given his experience with concentration camp survivors and refugees, he has probably in the back of his head the aftershocks from World War II. On July 4, in Kielce, Poland, a mob apparently egged on by the nascent Communist government attacks two hundred Jews who survived the Holocaust, killing forty-two: anti-Semitism survives. On July 22 in Jerusalem, the militant Irgun bombs the King David Hotel, headquarters of the British administration, and kills ninety-one. It's a bloody milestone on the road to creation of Israel.

I suspect my father would like to help in some way, but how? Since he's getting married, it's easy to say no to appeals to join groups trying to smuggle Jews into Palestine. The British authorities will allow only fifteen hundred a month, but several hundred thousand who survived the Nazis want to go. He has an offer to teach both children's and adult education classes at Malden Hebrew School: he could do his part that way, bonding them to Jewish civilization and inspiring them to support Zionist causes.

The next week my father tells Harvard's graduate school that he's newly married and will delay the start of his graduate studies by one semester: He'll be there in January 1947. Meanwhile, he'll teach at Malden Hebrew School.

In three straight semesters—spring and fall, 1947, and spring, 1948—he starts Assyrian and drops it after two weeks. He also drops a course in Arabic and never signs up for courses on "Markedness in Canaanite and Hebrew Verbs," "The Modal System of Old Babylon," and "Eighth-Century Iraqi Grammar." The presupposition is exactly what he wrote in his senior thesis: the Bible is from the ancient Near East, not from God. But I suspect that in his heart he wonders if that's right.

The recommendation he and his father wrote a dozen years earlier is prophetic: "If interested in a subject he is very tenacious. . . . Eli has but one fault if it can be called a fault, he has a gift for composing poetry and stories, and often spends too much time on the academic subjects which relate to those points which interest him, neglecting technical subjects."

The new Mrs. Olasky says he should continue with graduate school. My father does not tell her about his ouster from anthropology and the limited opportunities for someone with a master's degree in Semitic studies. She wouldn't understand academic politics, nor is she interested in news from Germany like the attempt by members of "Nakam" (the Hebrew word for "revenge") to inject arsenic into three thousand loaves of black bread baked in Nuremberg for German prisoners of war, including many SS members who committed war crimes. More than two thousand fall ill and 207 are hospitalized, but none die.

October 1946 brings two milestones. The hanging in Nuremberg of ten Nazi leaders. An Olasky pregnancy. My father celebrates both.

# 6

# It's an Unrespected Life

I'm trying hard to get into the January 1947 mindset of newly married Eli Olasky with a child due in six months. He's a different person from the one in January 1937 who fought for his college career when he was close to flunking out. He's unsure of himself and often passive.

The acronym PTSD was unknown in World War II, but one-tenth of mobilized American men spent time in hospitals for mental disturbances called "shell shock" or "soldier's heart." My father was in the front lines not of fighting but transporting displaced persons. His experiences with anti-Semitic bullies in Roxbury would not have prepared him to witness genocide.

The plot of the 1946 film *It's a Wonderful Life* has Jimmy Stewart's character several times on the brink of leaving Bedford Falls. But his willingness to help others traps him, and the dialogue of those watching him goes like this: "I know, I know, he didn't go." "That's right." In the movie he's frustrated, but he has the love and respect of his wife and community. Few things are better than that. Not having either can be psychologically crippling.

I have one document my father wrote about the goals of a Hebrew school. He listed three: "To enrich the character

69

and personality of the Jewish child through contact with the significant elements of his Jewish cultural heritage; to provide opportunities for meaningful religious experience by participation in holiday preparations and programming; and to promote in the child the desire to preserve the unity and integrity of Jewish community life."

None of those three mentions God, but they are consistent with the teaching of Mordecai Kaplan and with the desire to rebuild after the Holocaust. I suspect he discusses these goals with Malden Rabbi Jacob Lifshitz, who encourages him to teach at Malden Hebrew School: *We could use the prestige of having a Harvard graduate. Parents and children will respect an intellect like yours.*

Maybe that's true, maybe not, but he increasingly lacks respect from one crucial observer. My mother does not encourage him. On her wedding day she expected her new husband to receive advanced degrees from Harvard, become an anthropologist, and travel the world with her. But the possibility of Harvard recedes further once a second child, me, arrives in 1950. My father needs to earn dollars that are hard to come by in Hebrew school teaching.

Malden Hebrew School is a deliberately insular place, but sometimes the outside world comes knocking. On February 21, 1951, two politically ambitious members of his Harvard class of 1940 speak at Malden Hebrew School. One is Torbert Macdonald, a Malden boy who captained Harvard's football team in 1940. He won a Silver Star as a PT boat commander in the southwest Pacific and is now a lawyer seeking a seat in the House of Representatives. The other speaker, John F. Kennedy, was Macdonald's roommate. Also a medal-winning PT boat commander, he is now a congressman from Boston. Pundits expect him to run for the

Senate in 1952; it will be an uphill battle against the incumbent, Henry Cabot Lodge, Jr.

I suspect Beth Israel rabbi Charles Weinberg prods my father forward: *I don't know if you had any classes together, but Eli Olasky, our distinguished teacher here, graduated from Harvard the same year as you two—cum laude.* I picture Kennedy, smiling and saying, "That's impressive, Eli. I was just a jock. What house were you in?" My father mumbles, "I wasn't in a house. Dudley Hall." Kennedy grins and says, *Congratulations on the cum laude. The discussions you had in Dudley must have been something. That's where the brain trust was.*

I'm reading Kennedy's comments that day, a copy of which now reside in his presidential library in south Boston. He speaks about World Brotherhood, in capital letters, and of how "the things of the spirit can triumph over the thrust of communism and materialism. We know that the split atom and split mankind cannot long coexist on the same planet. But it will take all our energies to heal the breach." Kennedy calls for "a Brotherhood that says, 'I am going to respect you and invite you to respect me.'"

My father wants respect from his wife but doesn't get it. If he's not going to write books about anthropology, she wants him to write books about Judaism and become famous that way. The topic doesn't matter: she will help by typing the final version of his manuscripts, book publishers will bid on it, many people will buy it, and maybe my father can be on the new thing, television.

He doesn't write, although he's a good writer. PTSD? Hard to write what he believes when it is so different from the Orthodoxy of his father? Look how Mordecai Kaplan is treated, although he's a distinguished and degreed professor. Won't a lowly Hebrew school teacher be castigated? Only a smattering of synagogues or temples followed Reconstructionism's strange combination of not following the Bible but trying to uphold what was based on the Bible. My father would be unemployable.

Or perhaps he has nothing to say. I don't know, but my mother, in her disappointment, nags him more. She had married an intellectual, unlike her sisters who married men on their way to millionaire status. *Go out and give speeches!* I'm looking at a note from 1954, when he takes her advice and becomes one of three panelists in a discussion of Jewish education at Hebrew Teachers College.

In it, an Orthodox rabbi opposes sending children to public schools. He wants five-day-a-week Orthodox day schools that emphasize the study of Talmud and the practice of Talmudic law, halacha. He scorns those who say it's recreating European ghetto separatism: *See what good participation in German culture did for our people there.*

A Reform principal proposes dumping most traditions so as to make the connection to Israel the prime way of bonding youth to the Jewish people. He favors creation of a national bar mitzvah club that thirteen-year-olds should join, with their dues for three years going into a fund that they can tap at age sixteen to pay for a trip to Israel.

My father, without identifying himself denominationally, emphasizes teaching the last two thousand years of Jewish history and customs, along with Hebrew language instructions. Then comes a hard question: Must those who teach the Bible believe it? My father quotes Joshua Fishman from the 1952 winter issue of *Jewish Education*, "How seriously . . . should we want our children to take the supernatural aspects of the Bible? The answer is—just as seriously as we ourselves take them."

That's dodging the question, so my father raises a practical point. If only believers in the Bible as complete truth can be teachers, many classrooms will be empty. He quotes Moshe Greenberg in *Studies in the Bible and Jewish Thought*: "To carry out his duty the teacher is not required to assent personally to the answers given by the Bible."

I don't find records of any further speechifying.

As her sisters become queens of diamonds, my mother is depressed that the Harvard ace she grabbed has made her a two of clubs. Later, she tells me the story of her own mother, who became deeply depressed and ended her life saying, "a half century without love is enough."

That tale begins with a matchmaker proposing a match to a Jewish immigrant in Boston. How about marrying Miriam Weisman, a young woman from "the old country"? She is the daughter of Simon Weisman and Ida Krasnepolski (translation: beautiful resident of Poland), and is as lovely as her mother's name suggests. The immigrant in Boston will pay travel expenses plus the matchmaker's fee.

Deal: Miriam makes the long trip across Germany and the Atlantic. She arrives in Boston and Americanizes her name to Mollie. Then comes the informal inspection from her prospective husband. He takes one look at my grandmother and decides he doesn't want her. He bellows about matchmaker deception: *Krasivaya?* No, *Upodlivaya!* Not beautiful, ugly. Big teeth, chunky body. No marriage. (God was a far superior matchmaker. He brought Eve to Adam, who exclaimed, "Bone of my bones, and flesh of my flesh.")

Enter Robert Green, a barely literate mattress-maker in want of a wife. Was Mollie Green built to have babies? Yes. Was she a bargain? Yes: travel expenses already paid. On August 16, 1906, Mollie, shocked to be turned down, marries Robert Green on the rebound. He is interested only in work, and in having a wife to make meals and to produce children who can work for him once they become teenagers.

Mollie comes through, giving birth to eight children in thirteen years. One is stillborn, one dies as a baby, but six survive (and live to be ninety years old or more). Four of them, plus an eventual son-in-law, work at the business Robert Green starts, United Bedding. As the years go by, Mollie's life gets worse. My grandfather is psychologically and sometimes physically cruel. She adopts a habit that lasts for years: she boils a fresh chicken every night, and throws away leftovers the next day. Robert gets revenge by treating her much as the Cossacks had treated him.

At this point, when my mother is telling me this story, I interrupt: "What's this about Cossacks?" She says "that's not important," and goes on to describe her mother sitting silently on a chair in the corner of the kitchen, saying nothing. Later in life Mollie Green has shock treatments. She spends much of the day lying in bed, sometimes sleeping, sometimes groaning. She finally "turns her face to the wall" and decides not to eat any more. The official cause of death is heart failure, but my mother says Mollie starves herself to death.

In 1956 my parents have their tenth wedding anniversary, but my mother doesn't feel like celebrating. Her frustrations grow: Small apartment. Never money to go anywhere. I don't think my father ever sits down with her and speaks of the corpses and the crawling mostly-dead he had seen in Germany: Why give her nightmares as well? I doubt if they talked about what probably happened to their grandparents, cousins, and other relatives who had remained behind in Ukraine and Lithuania.

Instead, he tries to reason: *We have our own apartment now. We have food and heat and clothing. Life is full of tsoris,* suffering. Sometimes he proceeds along the lines of Rabbi Pinchas of Korets: "The root of gloominess is pride. An arrogant person thinks the world owes him honor and respect. He always feels slighted, believing that people disdain and snub him. As a result, he always is in a somber mood. A humble man cheerfully accepts everything that comes his way."

When my father throws sentences like that at my mother, she throws glasses or cups at him. She thinks he's high in IQ and low in DQ, determination quotient. She screams, "I'm not going to end up like my mother." He goes into a different room and sits there, reading, which infuriates her even more. But he does apply for jobs as a principal, not just a teacher. After ten years at Malden Hebrew School, my father becomes principal of the school newly created by Temple Israel in Natick, a growing city west of Boston.

That begins a dizzying stretch of eighteen years in at least six different suburban Boston synagogues and schools—Peabody and Swampscott to the north, Newton and Waltham to the west, and Natick and Needham southwest of Boston—plus one in Florida. My mother leaves three of them off the resumes she types. She also fudges the dates so my father's career isn't a succession of *two, three, I don't like thee*. But he knows he can't hold a principal's job very long. She knows too.

Almost every new position begins with an announcement to the congregation and sometimes a small story in the local newspaper. My mother saves articles with excited headlines: "Harvard Man to Become Hebrew School Principal." "JFK Classmate Heads Hebrew School." "From Harvard to Hebrew School." If a Harvard man can't convince members that Hebrew school is important, who can?

During the 1960s, Jewish education becomes a declining industry. Faith in God animates people. Apart from that, a focus on Jewish history and customs, and the study of the Hebrew language, has little appeal among increasingly secularized and often agnostic or atheistic Jews. Many parents still like bar mitzvah ceremonies as coming-of-age celebrations and opportunities to show off newly gained wealth. Many thirteen-year-olds like the loot that comes in from relatives. If necessary, the thirteen-year-old can read Hebrew prayers and Bible passages in transliteration, and guests may never know that Hebrew is Greek to him.

Facing declining enrollments, rabbis and school boards often conclude that a more entertaining curriculum and teaching style will save the day. Fritz Rothschild, a Jewish Theological Seminary professor, writes, "It is customary to blame secular science and anti-religious philosophy for the eclipse of religion in modern society. It would be more honest to blame religion for its own defeats. Religion declined not because it was refuted, but because it became irrelevant, dull, oppressive, insipid."

Novelist Harry Kemelman shows how that theory worked out practically in his popular 1960s series of Rabbi Small Mysteries. The books are set in a suburban Massachusetts city like many in which my father's career flames out. Here's Kemelman's depiction of a character with the jobs my father cycles through: "There was a rap on the door, and without waiting to be invited, in came Morton Brooks, the principal of the religious school. He was a bouncy, youngish man of forty, with a kind of theatrical flamboyance about him." Kemelman would probably have described my father as a somber, oldish man in his forties and fifties who stoically stares into space.

In Kemelman's book, Principal Brooks tells the rabbi, "You would be wise to pay a little more attention to the politics in the congregation. . . . The High Holidays are once a year . . . but the school—the kids go three times a week, and they report anything that happens the minute they get home. . . . Any little slight or fancied unfairness, you'd think from the way the parents carry on it was a pogrom."

Kemelman's principal then explains his brainstorm for a performance at a communal Passover meal: "'We could act it out, see.' . . . With tiny steps, he approached the rabbi's desk. . . . 'We'd modernize it and have [a teenager] say something like, "Golly, this is groovy, Dad."' . . . Maybe we could have another teen dressed as a hippie—you know, barefoot with beads and long hair and faded blue jeans. He [would say], "Hey, how come you cats snazzied up your pad like this? Crazy, man, crazy."'"

Kemelman's heroic rabbi vetoes the principal's suggestion, but the informal job description many school board leaders have for my father goes like this: *to amuse kids enough to get them to thirteen without rebelling, with the minimal knowledge to bluff through the last service they'll attend.*

My father takes Reconstructionism seriously. He wants his students to learn Hebrew, to bond with Jewish culture. Reconstructionist thinking appeals to some intellectuals. Reform Jews, though, aren't interested in maintaining ancient customs. Conservative Jews see Reconstructionists baking not a cake but a doughnut with a hole in the middle where belief in God should be. I know my father has theological debates with the rabbi at the temple where I'm bar mitzvahed. And where he does get along with the rabbi, school board members resent his lack of interest in schmoozing and his tendency to talk down to them, since they don't have the education he has.

I've skipped by the one time during the 1950s and 1960s when my parents try to declare independence from their memories. The getaway begins on July 4, 1957, when a Cadillac hearse leads a procession—I picture a Chevrolet Bel Air, Dodge Meadowbrook, Hudson Hornet, Crosley station wagon, Chrysler Plymouth Fury, and my parents' Nash Rambler—along a narrow West Roxbury road on either side of which sit forty-two small Jewish cemeteries. Some of the names: Boylston Lodge, Custom Tailors, Kehillath Jacob, Quincy Hebrew, Shepetovka, and Vilno. Many have chapel buildings that could be one-room schoolhouses, except for their stained glass windows and ornate chandeliers.

This is not an Independence Day parade. The cars head to a cemetery where Robert Green owns two plots. Today his abused wife Mollie Green, seventy-one years old, is being buried in area LI, grave 10. All six children and their spouses show up.

Justice of the Peace James O'Fallon had married Robert and Mollie in 1906, since they had no strong Jewish beliefs and were not connected to a synagogue in the strange land of America. A half century later they still have no synagogue membership, so a rabbi who has never previously met the Green family has the difficult task of commenting on the Greens' fifty-one years of wedded bliss. He trots out the clichés: "Their golden anniversary last year was the culmination of a long and loving marriage."

Robert Green goes home for a nap. His six children and their spouses go to the home of the oldest, Hymie. Some "loving marriage," he sneers. "He abused her."

Hymie says, "I remember him yelling, *Du farkirtst mir di yorn!* [You'll be the death of me.] She waves a broom at him and shrieks, *Gey strashe di gens!* [Go threaten the geese.]" The brothers and sisters groan, but they can't keep from laughing.

Celia recalls, "But he knocks aside the broom and calls her an *alte makhsheyfe* [old witch]. Remember his curses?

78

*Lign in drerd un bakn beygl!*" (A loose translation: "Lie on the ground on a place so hot—hell—that your body will bake bagels.")

Hymie adds, "Ma screamed back, *Nem Zich a vaneh!* [Go jump in the lake!]"

The laughter is louder, but my mother then says, "You were older. I was so scared in the bedroom." She then retreats into herself. Her sisters are remembering the past, but she's thinking of the future: Her husband never hits her or hollers at her, but—except for the Yiddish—some of those fighting words aren't all that different from what goes on in her house. Except she's usually the aggressor. The post-funeral discussion increases her resolve: *We have to get away from here.*

On the way home from the post-funeral discussion, my father and mother decide he should accept a job offer to become principal of Temple Beth Sholem in Hollywood, Florida. A new, growing Jewish community. My mother can get out from under the thumb of her father and leave all those memories behind. My father sees this as an opportunity to gain two things he wants: respect from wife and respect in his career.

# 7

# The Unkindest Cuts of All

My father's hopes are not realized. My mother is even less content in Florida than in Massachusetts. Shared suffering has created close bonds among her brothers and sisters. She misses them. She also misses when she throws shoes at scurrying palmetto bugs.

The 1960s for my mother is a decade of giving up expectations concerning her husband. She becomes a secretary. For twenty years, she types memos and letters for men not as smart as her, but our family has more money and she will have a pension. Tired of living in apartments, she inspects a few houses for sale, but the price is never right. Her weekly nagging fits become monthly. She invests her hope in her children: my brother and I will write the books and give the lectures she had hoped for from her husband.

My father, meanwhile, hops from school to school—but even if he is unsuccessful in becoming a beloved Mr. Chips of Jewish education, he hopes his children will be chips off the old block, doing their part to further Jewish civilization. That does not happen. My older brother becomes a fan of Friedrich Nietzsche and his atheism. I read hand-me-downs from him: *The Outline of History* by H. G. Wells, and Sigmund Freud's *The Future of an Illusion*.

Wells alludes to the Bible not with scorn but with condescending sympathy: "It is quite understandable that the Exodus story, written long after the events it narrates, may have concentrated and simplified, and perhaps personified and symbolized, what was really a long and complicated history of tribal invasions." My father suggested similar things in his senior thesis. Wells convinces me to think of the Bible as neither good nor evil, just antiquated.

Wells mocks the childlike awe of the Hebrews before Solomon's temple and palace, since "beside the beauty and wonder of the buildings and organizations of such great monarchs as Thotmes III . . . or Nebuchadnezzar the Great, they are trivial." Freud for me is a direct shot at Hebrew school teaching. I buy his notion that people invented God because "the terrifying impression of helplessness in childhood aroused the need for protection. . . . The recognition that this helplessness lasts through life made it necessary to cling to the existence of a father, but this time a more powerful one."

Aha! I now know from Freud, a very smart man, that religion is for children and God does not exist except as an imaginary Superdad—and since I'm not so impressed with dads except on television, I plan to do without another.

My father, following Mordecai Kaplan, has been saying for years that children growing up in a Jewish home, one that observes traditions like keeping kosher, will identify with Judaism not as a religion but a civilization. Maybe, but in our home all I see is my mother sometimes putting out candlesticks for Friday evening Shabbat dinners, followed by an unenthusiastic prayer to Someone who probably doesn't exist. We do proceed logically: Since Passover is a major holiday and Hanukkah a minor one, we proudly refuse to turn the latter into a gift-giving orgy just because the Christians do that at Christmas. I feel noble about that—but also sad.

My father wants me, post–bar mitzvah, to go to evening classes at a Hebrew high school two nights per week. I resist, grumbling each time. In October, claiming sickness, I put a thermometer under hot water to gain scientific backing. He's not fooled, but he grasps my animosity. With my Hebrew school days over, he says I should ask him questions.

The questions I decide to ask come with a tad of logic but a sneering tone: *Where's God in this? Why care about the Jewish cultural heritage if it's not centered on God?* But maybe I have a different grievance, in the manner of the fine movie *Indiana Jones and the Last Crusade.* Professor Henry Jones tells the archaeologist-hero Indiana, "I was a wonderful father. . . . I taught you self-reliance." Indiana's retort: "What you taught me was that I was less important to you than people who had been dead for five hundred years in another country."

When I'm fourteen I ask this: Given the amount of space given to the sacrificial system in Leviticus and other books of the Bible, how could it simply have ended two thousand years ago without God instituting something else to take its place? My father says he'll show me how the Talmudic authors deal with that, but I sneer: *You're saying that because you don't know the answer.*

I don't remember the exact words, but my sentences that follow include one or more of the following three—*foolish, idiotic, childish*—within a few words of God. My father, for the only time in our lives, slaps me. After that, he and I speak little. My mother also gives up. During my years from age thirteen to eighteen, my father is moving from teaching job to teaching job, often proving his worth by teaching adult evening classes, which means his workday runs from two o'clock in the afternoon to nine at night. Our eating together as a family becomes rare. Mostly we forage in the refrigerator and pantry.

Eight years after Mollie Green dies, Robert Green is buried next to her. Once again cars snake along a narrow West Roxbury road, but this time they are Cadillacs along with a Buick Riviera, a Lincoln, a Studebaker, and one Chevrolet Nova, ours. The death notice in the May 24, 1965, *Boston Globe* calls him a "devoted father" and says, "Contributions may be made to the charity of your choice."

Robert Green's six children and their spouses meet afterward at the home of the youngest, David. They scoff at the "devoted father" line. Hymie, the oldest, recalls a bitterly cold day during Prohibition when, walking home with bootleg liquor for his father, he sees a policeman and fears arrest. Hymie jumps over a stone fence but breaks the bottle. He smells of booze, fears the police will arrest him, but also fears returning without the bottle. The threat of frostbite finally pushes him home. Robert Green takes off his belt and whips him with it again and again.

All twelve grab another cigarette: Kents, most of them. As smoke swirls through the living room, Hymie talks about how the dear departed refused to let him study to become a lawyer: "I have ulcers because of him." Celia, the eldest daughter, says, "He wanted me to be his little rumrunner, but I said no. He slapped me so hard I flew across the room." The next daughter, Bessie, says, "You all know I take lithium. It's because of him." Edith says, "You know why it says 'charity of your choice.' Because he was charitable only to his own pocket."

The two youngest adults put up a half-hearted defense. David says, "Look, he worked hard. It's not easy to move into the middle class from where he started, and most of us have done better." My mother says, "He taught us good lessons. Everyone is out to get you. Don't trust anyone."

It turns out that Robert Green's will isn't clear. The six couples fight over the inheritance. Their family bridge games stop, and half don't talk with the other half for almost a decade.

Three months later my mother is still listening to Metropolitan Opera radio broadcasts on Saturday afternoons. She looks forward to a special program the evening of September 16, 1965, because the company is inaugurating its new home at Lincoln Center.

My mother, in the kitchen, listens to Milton Cross as he waxes rhapsodic about all the celebrities present for the grand opening: Lady Bird Johnson with Philippine President Ferdinand Marcos and his wife Imelda, Senators Robert and Ted Kennedy and their wives, Governor Nelson Rockefeller and Mayor John Lindsay, Estée Lauder, and four thousand others.

Cross describes the new hall: elegantly curving staircases, gold circles in the ceiling and on the fronts of scalloped boxes, dazzling chandeliers, royal red carpet. He exclaims about the production itself, the world premiere of *Antony and Cleopatra* by Barber and Zeffirelli, and the beauty of Leontyne Price's soprano voice, which could be silky or raspy.

My mother says she has listened for years but has never been there in person. She would love to go someday. She looks over at my father, reading a science fiction novel. He hows no reaction. Maybe he didn't hear her. I go to my bedroom and listen to the Red Sox game on WHDH. My brother has gone to college at the University of Chicago.

That becomes another story of disappointment for my mother. Sidney scores well on the Merit Scholarship test late in 1964. My mother learns that the World Book encyclopedia company sponsors Merit Scholarships for employees' children. She becomes an employee by selling five World Book sets, several to sisters and brothers. It pays off in April 1965 when the University of Chicago accepts Sidney, and he becomes a Merit Scholar. None of her sisters or brothers have a child with such an illustrious title at such an illustrious school.

Six months after Sidney enters college he drops out. My father puts aside his antipathy to travel and flies with my mother to Chicago in an unsuccessful attempt to convince Sidney to stay. I go with them and enjoy looking around Chicago.

Sidney has not taken into account the escalating war in Vietnam and the escalating needs of the US Army for infantry soldiers. He spends the summer of 1966 at basic training in Fort Dix, New Jersey. Ida Olasky feels great concern as a mother but is also embarrassed in relation to those sisters and brothers who have done her a favor by buying encyclopedias. Her sudden drop from A to F in the overall competition concerning children's accomplishments is depressing.

Throughout the turmoil concerning his eldest son, my father seems to be a stoic, as usual—but several months later, at age forty-nine, he has what my mother calls a "mild" heart attack, and another "mild" one two years later. I do not offer any comfort. He cuts back on his cigarette smoking and moves exclusively to a pipe. Ida cuts back on her screaming and moves to softer belittlements.

That is an improvement, but she also starts to warble repeatedly the nostalgic theme song from the world's longest running musical ever, *The Fantasticks*, which begins its New York career in 1960 and keeps chugging until 2002. At least nine popular singers—Patti Page, Andy Williams, Perry Como, Liza Minnelli—make its song their own, as does my mother, day after day: "Try to remember the kind of September / When life was slow . . ."

Any sympathy I offer is hollow. I wonder whether she is going crazy, with the strain of Sidney pushing her over the brink. He's in the rice paddies in March 1967 as a private in the First Air Cavalry, which suffers more "killed in action" (5,444) in Vietnam than any other US army division. Saigon military briefers reveal the US body count each week and say more Vietcong or North Vietnamese soldiers have died. That does not comfort my parents.

We spend dinnertime in front of the television, watching news shows. We eat on trays and let news anchors and reporters do the talking. I walk or bicycle to school, get books from the library, and read throughout the weekends. From Monday to Friday, I stay late after school to work on the high school newspaper and yearbook, get home just in time for dinner, and after dinner barricade myself in my bedroom, its walls covered with maps. I come out only to watch television.

Sidney survives, returns to the United States, and legally changes his name to Jason. I go to Yale. During the summer, I work as a day camp counselor and then a *Boston Globe* reporter, gaining praise from editors for being not only willing but also eager to spend more than thirty-five hours per week in the city room or out reporting—anywhere but home.

Just as Ida has looked forward to spending a twenty-fifth

reunion week at Harvard, so she has dreamed of a son marching in cap and gown at a Yale graduation. Instead, in 1971 I wear jeans and a placard supporting Yale dining hall workers on strike.

The following year my father starts doing income tax returns with H&R Block. My mother still hopes he will get a job in public education, so she pushes him to get some recommendations from where he has taught. One from Temple Shalom in Newton: "He was most reliable in fulfilling assigned tasks. As you know, he is a Harvard graduate." One from the chairman of the Temple Beth El school committee: "He is a fine Hebrew scholar. He left us in order to undertake a more broadening experience in administration at Middlesex Community College."

Not exactly true. His job at Temple Beth El ends in the spring of 1974. He is unemployed for a year and then takes the position at Middlesex, but it is not a real job. His supervisor there says he is in a position "funded from the CETA program, it was what I would call apprenticeship training . . . in areas such as admissions, fiscal control . . . and in the area of physical plant equipment control."

CETA, the Comprehensive Employment and Training Act, creates temporary jobs for individuals in three main categories: long-term unemployed, low-income employed, and high school students who need summer work. A 1982 Congressional Budget Office study of the program notes, "Participants in CETA training programs are members of low-income families." Median family income is $5,000.

Most CETA apprentices are studying to gain high school equivalency degrees or to become clerical workers. Clearly, my father is not the target population for CETA, but Middlesex administrators give him an internship, figuring he might help rather than haunt them. My father answers phones, files reports, maintains files, schedules appointments, and delivers internal mail.

Looking back, I'm impressed that he doesn't stay home. He has the humility to take a welfare-to-work job. I'm in graduate school when he loses his last Hebrew school teaching job. I don't know anything about that, but I don't ask. Sadly, he's a real-life Rodney Dangerfield, getting no respect from his wife or children. The only organization that will employ him is one that gets him for free.

My father when he looks in the mirror sees someone who never came through on his early promise. In the 1981 edition of *Wealth and Poverty*, George Gilder writes, "Like welfare, CETA often has the effect of shielding people from the realities of their lives and thus prevents them from growing up and finding or creating useful tasks." For my parents, probably the opposite is true. CETA certifies my father's failure and my mother's scorn.

Maybe the unkindest cut of all comes in May 1976. My parents' latest apartment has a dining room table. I bring for a visit the woman I plan to marry the next month. She has grown up in Royal Oak, Michigan, the daughter of a Ford middle manager.

I anticipate some unease when announcing at dinner that Susan and I will get married. I do not comprehend my father's gut-twisting feeling as he gets up from the table, walks away, and doesn't appear the rest of the evening. Susan is smart, pretty, and utterly delightful in every way. What's not to like?

For my father, first and most important is that she is not Jewish. But I suspect secondary factors also affect him: Her father is a career employee of the company built by Henry Ford, the twentieth century's leading anti-Semitic corporate boss. She's from Royal Oak, home of twentieth-century

America's biggest spreader of anti-Semitism, radio priest Charles Coughlin.

Maybe I'm not even thinking in those terms because I never studied the Holocaust, never felt any anti-Semitism, never faced the terror of traveling through enemy territory as my father had to do every day he went to Hebrew Teachers College. I was never beaten up by anti-Semites, as he probably was, or faced invidious discrimination and stereotyping in college.

Nor had I seen the institutionalized anti-Semitism that once pervaded the Roman Catholic Church. The Roman Catholic prelate in my consciousness was Richard Cardinal Cushing, who criticized anti-Semitism and anti-Semitic "lies . . . uttered in ordered to delude us." The Second Vatican Council in 1962 included some hierarchs who had winked at the "blood libel," the idea that Jews at Passover killed Christian children and baked matzohs with blood. At that gathering, Cushing called all to love Jews as "the blood brothers of Christ."

Despite his unhappiness, my father comes with my mother to our wedding in Royal Oak.

The next year brings an even bigger blow that I deliver from my teaching post in California: Susan and I have both become Christians.

I'm sure my explanations of what that means are not satisfactory. "Why are you adopting your wife's religion?" (I'm not. Susan, coming from a very liberal United Methodist background, had to come as far as I did in gaining faith in Christ.) "And what will you teach your children?" (They will grow up learning about Abraham, Moses, David, and all the biblical leaders, which is much more than they'd get if I remained an atheist.)

The ghosts of Christian activities past fill my parents' thinking. Why are you joining the Roman Catholics? (I'm not; I'm a Protestant.) But even concerning Roman Catholicism, here's what Cushing told fifteen hundred delegates of the Union of American Hebrew Congregations, meeting in Boston: "No man could have my faith concerning Christ without desiring to be more like Him and, therefore, seek and befriend all men without exception—white, black, Gentile, Jew."

My father departed from his father's Orthodoxy but remained within the big tent of Judaism. My grandfather departed from his parents geographically but remained within Orthodoxy. So my leap is larger, and since my father has apparently decided that for him belief in God (other than, maybe, a distant deistic god) is unimportant, it's hard for him to understand someone to whom it's crucially important. My previous atheism does not seem like personal rejection. This does.

Many new Christians have faced similar reactions over the centuries, and come to understand what Jesus said: "Whoever loves father or mother more than me is not worthy of me." But I can appreciate it's hard for my father. We have one conversation in which he states that the best translation of the Hebrew word "almah" in Isaiah 7:14 is "young woman," as Jewish scholars stipulate, rather than "virgin," as many Christian translations from the King James Version to the English Standard Version contend.

Maybe, but when I bring up information from a book first published in 1972, Josh McDowell's *Evidence That Demands a Verdict*, my father disengages. Nor does he show any interest in my personal story of coming to faith in Christ, but maybe I could have told it more effectively.

From 1978 to 1984, we exchange visits and occasional

letters or calls, but no meetings of mind or heart occur. Jews do not name babies after living ancestors, so my wife and I do not honor him in that way, but we show him one grandson in 1977 and another in 1980. Then smoking takes its toll: bladder cancer. My father dies in December 1984. In April 1985, my wife and I name our third son Daniel Eli.

# 8

# Beyond Scapegoats

"Deep in December, it's nice to remember," my mother warbles. I'm not sure it was nice for my father to remember. Did he have hope for eternal life? As far as I know, no. Did he have satisfaction in his marriage, his career, his children?

I examine some "comps." Starting in 1938, the Grant Study of Adult Development assesses every decade or so the physical, emotional, and career health of two hundred men who studied at Harvard between 1938 and 1944. The original researchers select men likely to lead "successful" lives: high IQs, good GPAs, recommendations from college deans.

Looking at outcomes sixty years later, I'm struck that all those advantages are no guarantee of success, especially in marriage. 20 percent of those still living have an intact and happy first marriage, 50 percent are (like my father) in a poor or so-so first marriage, and 21 percent are divorced. I'm grateful that my parents didn't divorce.

But some of the capsule biographies suggest a path out of sadness. For example, upper-class Algernon Young "started out with everything going for him. [Yet] much of his life was misery. . . . His life revolved around his pets, who kept him 'too busy' for other relationships. 'Catering to six cats can be a big affair,' he explained. He found engagement with other people demanding and frightening. . . . His renascence began at 51, when he gave up the agnosticism he had maintained."

My father had no renascence. Should I blame Harvard, because what my father learned at Harvard undermined his early faith in God? Should I blame Kaplan for offering bad theology, or the suburban Judaism that demanded entertainment rather than serious study? Should I blame myself for not being a better son, and later not presenting the gospel more winsomely? God's sovereignty does not eliminate our personal responsibility, so we could say that all of us reaped what we sowed.

Had my mother been supportive rather than disappointed and critical, my father's career might have been different. His life would certainly have been more pleasant. God has blessed me with a supportive wife, so I feel sorry that my father did not have that satisfaction and help. A widow for twenty-four years, my mother sometimes said she was just trying to help her husband. She sometimes asked how anyone could expect anything different from her, since she had a brutal father and never had a teddy bear, a birthday party, or even a bed of her own until she was twenty.

Does my cousin remember my mother as "the angriest woman" because of the angry man buried on May 23, 1965, in area I, grave 9, West Roxbury Independent Workmen's Circle? Was Robert Green the person responsible for his wife's misery, which contributed to my mother's misery, which contributed to my father's?

My mother spoke of the role of the Cossacks in her father's life. Here's what I've put together from what she and cousins told me about Robert Green's forced military service in the czar's army, desertion, betrayal, and eventual escape. I'm adding details from Russian military histories and memoirs.

Let's start with what the genealogical records reveal: Reuben Grin, born in 1883, grows up in Bobruisk, Russia, a mostly Jewish city of thirty-five thousand persons famed for a fortress that repels Napoleon's army for four months in 1812. By the 1880s it is no longer in use, so children like Reuben play at soldiering there. They march up and down, dreaming of seeing far-away places.

Bobruisk is famous for its military parades. Reuben watches and hears a magnificent band playing the imperial Russian anthem. The brass instruments shine, the silver trumpets sing, the timpani booms—all far more magnificent than Jewish klezmer bands with their violins and clarinets. Then come the riders, four strong horses abreast, preening down the street—not the swaybacks of the shtetl, Reuben's Jewish neighborhood.

None of that prepares Reuben for the turn-of-the-century scene at the draft induction center. Day after day, according to accounts, mothers wail and hug their suspiciously deficient sons. Some have dislocated fingers and broken toes. One eighteen-year-old only has one ear. With wars on the horizon, some parents will do almost anything to help their sons to avoid six years of immediate service and nine years in the reserve.

Reuben is there with his mother, Tobe ("God is good") Hasmonikon. That last name means a claimed descent from the Hasmonean dynasty that ruled Israel 2,100 years ago. But if that was so, the family has certainly fallen on hard times: Reuben has grown up poor and illiterate, never with a bed or toys of his own. I imagine him picturing himself in a new soldier's uniform featuring double-breasted jackets with colored piping.

For hours Reuben sits and watches differential treatment. Non-Jews who pass their physicals receive permission to return home for a month before reporting. A Jew considered fit for service emerges from the examining room with a guard who hustles him to a wagon for immediate transport to an army base.

Tobe sits quietly, and Reuben thinks the mothers of other Jews at the induction center are overdoing it. When a clerk calls his name, I picture him standing in line with a dozen others. The young man in front of Reuben coughs. He seems hardly able to walk. When the military examiner says, "You'll do. Army bread will make you healthy," he collapses and his mother screams. Two soldiers carry him out.

Reuben is solidly built and has no trouble with his physical testing, but the examiner is suspicious: "Why aren't you trying to avoid service like all the others? Are you a revolutionary?" Reuben denies any such interest. "My father, Yudl, sits all day making mattresses. I want a different life."

The examiner chuckles. "You want a different life? That we can guarantee." Reuben signs a paper in Russian that he can't read. His mother, still stolid, hands him a bag containing boiled potatoes and kasha. A guard walks him to a *fura*, a canvas-covered wagon with a troika of horses and a dozen draftees inside. "Where are we going?" Reuben asks. The reply: "You'll find out."

Soon, Reuben does, and he's horrified. He becomes a Fourth Army Corps blacksmith in the Fourth Cavalry Division of the Cossacks. For a Jew, Cossacks are the worst. For 250 years Jewish fathers left a lasting impression on their sons by describing a seventeenth-century Cossack uprising led by Bohdan Khmelnytsky, who buried Jews alive and cut them to pieces.

For Reuben, if his situation is typical, service among the

Cossacks means every-hour summons—"Jewish dog, do this"—with beatings if he does not instantly respond with quivering bows. Reuben's father Yudl is not deeply religious, but Reuben still gags as he learns to force down the Russian army staple: pork. And what about seeing the world? Reuben sees mostly the back ends of horses and mules. He feels daily chagrin. *What a fool I was.*

By the spring of 1902, Reuben has had enough. Other young men his age are heading to America. Some desert to do so, walking mostly by night or riding in a carefully chosen wagon to the German border, and then going faster by train and boat. But they all need some money.

In today's dollars, the cost of a Russia-to-America trip is typically $2,000: Travel to Germany and payment to a border smuggler: $300. Ocean travel from Hamburg or Bremen to Liverpool, and then belowdecks passage to New York City: $925. Food and hostel stays at exit ports: $150. Money to show American officials that the immigrant will not start off as a pauper: $625. Living in America: priceless.

So when Reuben finally summons the courage to desert, he heads home to raise funds from family members and neighbors. Surely they will help him to get away. But they do not: the Bobruisk fire of 1902 has devoured the homes of 2,500 families, as well as 250 businesses, the city market and library, the Jewish hospital, and fifteen synagogues and schools. Reuben pleads: his life is in danger! Friends and relatives say no. *We need the money for our own survival and for rebuilding.*

Reuben bitterly comes to one conclusion: don't rely on friends and relatives. His desperate plan now: head to Wilna (now Vilnius), two hundred miles west of Bobruisk and not far from the Russia-Germany border. Jews make up one-half of the 160,000 population of Wilna, so someone will surely help him there. It also has a famous synagogue-run soup kitchen where he could get free meals.

I suspect Reuben for a week walks much of the way there, often traveling by cold night, sometimes diving into carts going his way, always looking around to see if a bounty hunter seeking a payday is out to capture a Jewish deserter.

Coming into Wilna and proud to make it that far, Reuben asks for directions to the soup kitchen. A middle-aged man with a kind smile volunteers to guide him. As they walk, the man asks Reuben what had happened to his *payot*, the curly sidelocks most Jews wear. Reuben offers a comment about changing fashions. The man compliments Reuben on his strong boots: "Looks like you could fight a battle in them." Reuben smiles.

It starts to rain. The kind-looking man says, "Please come to my house, dry off, and have something to eat." Reuben agrees. The man takes him up into a two-story house with a side lot pasturing three horses and a cow. They enter a wallpapered room with silver-framed mirrors on the wall. It is so different from his one-story Bobruisk home, little more than a hut, that Reuben stares and says, "I'd like to have a home like this someday."

Suddenly two men in uniform burst into the house. "He's a deserter," the man who guided him says. The others grab Reuben. Terror takes over his brain, then his bowels—and then nothing. I suspect he wakes up with a giant lump on his head and a bad smell. He is in a *fura* heading east. His guards give him nightly whippings: "Preparation for the big one," they say.

Soon Reuben is back among the Cossacks. If his punishment is typical, Reuben receives thirty official lashes each month—plus every soldier feels free to kick him. Reuben's back is a checkerboard of lacerations, his thighs a pyramid of bruises. Every time he bends to his blacksmithing, he aches. Reuben suffers weeks of systematic beatings and treatment as subhuman, and he hopes his Cossack captors eventually will recognize him as a human being. They do not, but he watches them fight each other with knives—whoever draws first blood wins—and learns winning tactics.

In the summer of 1903, Reuben deserts once again. This time he does not ask for money: he robs merchants at knifepoint. Reuben manages to evade arrest and makes it to Eydtkuhnen on the German border. There, a smuggler guides him across the border: 80 percent of Russian emigrants, and 100 percent of deserting soldiers, leave illegally. He uses the name Rachmiel Menikov, in case one of the czar's bloodhounds tries a cross-border snatch.

First comes train travel in a sealed cattle car—room for eight horses or thirty-two persons—from the Russian-German border to Ruhleben, near Berlin. (Germans worry about immigrants bringing disease.) The odor of bodies and of strong Russian tobacco often makes travelers gag. At Ruhleben, officials inspect, delouse, and disinfect all baggage.

Then comes a second shock: Emigrants have to take off all their clothes and walk into a closed room. Some suspect murder as the doors close. They receive a shower of hot water instead. (Later, the Nazis would also force Jews into sealed rooms—and poison gas would descend from the ceiling.)

Next, another sealed train takes emigrants to barracks of the Hamburg-America Line in Hamburg or the North German Lloyd in Bremen. In both cities, doctors inspect passengers for telltale signs of disease: if they cross the Atlantic and officials do not allow them entry into the

United States, the steamship companies have to cover all costs of an involuntary return journey.

Reuben buys a steerage ticket that entitles him to a floor space in the ship's hold. He sleeps alongside hundreds of others amid—according to a report of the US Immigration Commission—"the unattended vomit of the seasick, the odors of not-too-clean bodies, the reek of food and the awful stench of the nearby toilet rooms." But no one whips him.

My grandfather arrives in Boston by ship on December 3, 1903. He is one of a group of thirty pushed onto the top deck of a barge, with baggage below. He walks up a steep stairway. Doctors watch for heavy breathing that suggests a heart condition, a bewildered gaze that might show mental inability, or sores on faces, necks, and hands.

Doctors scrawl large white letters on the back of about one of every five immigrants: *B* for a possible back problem, *Sc* for scalp infection, *X* for possible mental defect. Marked men and women head to examining rooms. Others move on to scrutiny by "eye men" for symptoms of trachoma, which can cause blindness. They then record names: an official writes down Reuben Grin as Robert Green.

He first lives in Boston's North End, then stuffed with rows of three-story tenements. Almost all single men are boarders in two-bedroom apartments. A husband, wife, and children sleep in one room, and typically two boarders share a thin straw mattress on a metal frame or on the floor, in the second bedroom.

The kitchen is the most-used room. It has the only sink, so everyone washes there. The landlady uses it to wash her family's and the boarders' laundry. One toilet in the hall typically serves the four families on one floor plus the eight boarders.

The landlady cooks what becomes known as the standard "Jewish dinner": a piece of herring or chopped liver, some pea or barley soup, some cooked meat and plums accompanied by a pickle, and a glass of beer. Breakfast is typically black bread and coffee consumed while standing up.

It's a hard life, but he's not beaten. Besides, Robert Green formulates a business plan as he passes by shopkeepers in their doorways and Italian organ-grinders on streets crowded with pushcarts. His father, Yudl, has taught him about mattresses. Straw mattresses after years of use are dirty, uncomfortable, and often loaded with lice, fleas, and bed bugs. Wouldn't families and boarders sleep better and be happier if he fumigates and restuffs old ones?

Robert Green goes door-to-door, sometimes carrying four mattresses at a time on his strong back. His workday is sixteen hours, but he receives pay from satisfied customers when he returns their restuffed mattresses. He eventually moves up to a pushcart, then to a wagon drawn by a horse with three legs, and then to a four-legged one.

Robert Green can now afford Lucky Strikes and liquor. He goes from peddling used mattresses, to making new ones, to starting his own company—United Bedding—and opening up a furniture store in East Boston. His business survives a fire and burglaries. He doesn't forget how he started: fifty years after arriving in Boston he still sells used mattresses, for eight dollars each.

He moves seven miles north of Boston to a growing Jewish neighborhood in suburban Malden. He buys there a two-story house that, with some work, can be like the one he saw in Vilna. In its yard stand three horses and a cow. Later he buys another two-story house and rents out the first.

Even when he can afford more, Robert Green hates to

spend money. The four girls share one bedroom, two girls to a bed. All six children are smart, but they learn early that their job is to have full-time jobs immediately after high school. Robert Green, after his forced servitude to the Cossacks, has given up on God. He teaches his children not to "waste time" by reading the Bible.

My grandfather has courage and entrepreneurial ability, but he never forgets how he was brutalized. His maxim becomes, *Do unto others as they have done unto you.* His final material accomplishment before dying in 1965 is the purchase of a new lime-green Mercury. He never learns how to drive and no one else drives it, but the beautiful car sits in front of his house, showing all the neighbors that Robert Green's hardness has brought him success.

Scapegoating is an occupational hazard for writers of family history: It's easy to blame parents. I understand more about my father, now that I know about his experiences. I understand my mother more, now that I know more about her parents. If I report the ugly side of my maternal grandfather, am I dishonoring him? No, he reacted as he did to the brutality he experienced. The Cossacks who tortured him were responding to the way they were treated—which doesn't excuse bad behavior, but shows what even skeptics sometimes say is the leading empirical proof for a Christian worldview: the universality of sin.

The jagged history of humanity starts with original sin, which we might think of like the stacked turtles Bertrand Russell wrote about in 1927. Antonin Scalia in a 2006 opinion, *Rapanos v. United States,* offered a recent version of the tale: "An Eastern guru affirms that the earth is supported on the back of a tiger. When asked what supports the tiger, he says it stands upon an elephant. When asked what supports the elephant he says it is a giant turtle. When asked, finally, what supports the giant turtle, he is briefly taken aback, but quickly replies, 'Ah, after that it is turtles all the way down.'"

It's sin all the way down. We are naturally wretched, passing on original sin in ways that are sometimes creative but often repetitious. At first glance, an iron chain bonds together generation after generation. And I'm part of that chain. I've realized in the course of this research how self-centered I was, not only as a child but as an adult. Why did I have so little interest in seeing my parents not primarily as people to meet my needs (or not) but as individuals with their own struggles? I never really cared to find out about them.

Yet sometimes, with God's grace and mercy, that iron chain becomes a readily breakable daisy chain. Those who see the miraculous transition cry out joyfully, as the apostle Paul did, "Wretched man that I am! Who will deliver me from this body of death? Thanks be to God through Jesus Christ our Lord!" When we have faith in God we can look squarely at our own sin because nothing is a surprise to God. We learn that we're worse than we have imagined but more loved than we could have hoped for.

I've also realized in this process that I misinterpreted some things. All my cousins saw Robert Green as cold, but maybe he mellowed as he aged. Once, when my mother had me do addition and recite-the-alphabet-backward tricks, he said—as I heard it—"kehpin marble, marble." I had no idea what that meant, but one of my cousins decades later explained that, impressed with my show-off smartness, he was honoring me with a comic book title: "Captain Marvel, Marvin."

My father had a certain definition of what being a good father meant. He had resented pressure from his father to be a doctor, so he never pressured me about taking a certain course or going to a certain school. He had no car, but I grew up with access to a car and did not have to pay for it. He grew up poor during the Depression, but he made sure his family had a home and we never went hungry.

My mother had a certain definition of what being a good mother was. She made sure we had breakfasts, lunches, and dinners. My brother and I had what she never had: our own beds and some toys. A photo of four-year-old me shows me with a big teddy bear, and she never had even a small one. We went to college.

Relishing (and for many years misusing) the liberty they provided, I never thanked my father for that, and for the material things he and my mother provided. Like many of his generation, my father never spoke of his World War II experience. Like many of my generation, I didn't ask. I didn't honor him when he was alive, but I can tell his story now with appreciation for his sacrifices, and sadness about his sadness. Since my mother lived twenty-four years beyond his death, I was able to thank her.

And here's one last insight I gained only while writing this book, which led me to read more about World War II and its millions of innocent victims. What if, as I was growing up, my father had embedded in me the gruesome detail he probably saw while sweeping up the ruins of the Third Reich? What if he had told me how some of my great-grandparents probably received bullets in the head from Nazi soldiers and collaborators? Or even, regarding something short of murder but still hard: What if had regaled me with stories of his traveling to and from Hebrew Teachers College through hostile territory?

I grew up without consciousness of anti-Semitism. It was undoubtedly there, but I was unaware. What if my father had rat-a-tat-tatted into my brain a sense that the world was against me? For a decade in the late 1960s and early 1970s, I went seriously astray but retained an overall optimism unmarred by nightmares about Holocaust horrors. I regret as an adult not pressing my father further for information about his past, but I now see more method in his reticence.

I suspect my father, like a murder detective who doesn't tell his wife what he saw that day, also spared my mother the specific detail. But as those law-and-order TV shows have frequently informed us, there's a cost to the person who psychologically isolates himself to keep the virus of pessimism from spreading. My father was hostile to Christianity and its central theme of supreme sacrifice for others, but in this way, he was Christlike—and I belatedly thank him for that.

He was also wounded, as was my mother, as was her father, as were the Cossacks, as is everyone. But no wound is too deep for Christ to heal.

# Appendix

# How God Saved Me

P&R editors asked me to include my conversion experience and my father's reaction to it. He never gave me his reaction in words, but he did not believe that God intervenes in lives, so he expressed no interest in hearing how God had saved me. I did not persist in telling him the story, which I should have.

I will, though, tell about the experience here, because it is a manifestation of God's grace. In the fall of 1973, I was a graduate school Communist, winning compliments from professors who relished my Marxist analyses. To get a PhD, I had to have a good reading knowledge of a foreign language, so I was studying Russian by reading stories in *Pravda*, the Moscow newspaper, which called for "unyielding war against religious patterns of thought (which have no place alongside a materialistic world-view, social, scientific, and technical progress) and the suppressing, once and for all, of those relics from the past."

On November 1, All Saints Day, I walked on the University of Michigan campus and picked up a discarded Halloween mask of Richard Nixon. While eating a late lunch in the West Quad dining hall, I looked at Watergate-related headlines—"White House Says Two Key Tapes Don't

Exist," "Saxbe Named Attorney General." Then I returned to my room just off campus and sat in my red chair, reading Lenin's famous essay "Socialism and Religion."

In it Lenin wrote, "We must combat religion—this is the ABC of all materialism, and consequently Marxism." Following Marx, Lenin called religion "opium for the people. [It] is a sort of spiritual booze, in which the slaves of capital drown their human image." I had read this before, but a refresher was helpful. What happened next, from 3:00 p.m. to 11:00 p.m., was the strangest experience of my life. Since I had never taken LSD or hallucinated, I can rule out those possible explanations of why I sat in that chair for eight hours, looking at the clock each hour out of surprise that I still hadn't moved.

It seems mystical and I can't describe well the experience, but it reversed the course of my life. I felt myself walking in a dark corridor from which doors opened out on both sides. I felt along the walls and tried to open the doors, but they were all locked. Then I came to one that was slightly open. I paused before the door, opened it, and walked into the room. Suddenly an explosion of light allowed me to see everything in the room—but nothing was there except golden walls and a brightness.

Somehow I thought the brightness was God. Lenin's hatred for the "figment of man's imagination" called God was not new to me, but some surprising thoughts began battering my brain: What if Lenin was wrong? What if God does exist? What is my relationship to this God, if he's there? Why, when he is kind to me, do I offer evil in return?

From where were these thoughts coming? In my brain, Marxism was settled social science. What was happening to me? What were the implications of God's existence? I came down toward specifics: Is America fundamentally evil? If not, why am I turning my back on it? Why was capitalist desire for money and power worse than Communist desire? I had embraced treasonous ideas: Why? Louis Olasky had denounced the tsar. Why was I kissing up to a new one— Leonid Brezhnev, of all people?

It's hard for me to convey the strangeness of this experience. I have trouble sitting still during lectures. I like to walk while thinking, but I sat in the chair, hour after hour, suddenly realizing I was wrong to embrace Marx and Lenin. At 3:00 p.m., I was an atheist and a Communist. When I got up at 11:00 p.m., I was not. I had no new data but suddenly had, through a means I did not understand, a new way of processing data. Was I born again? No, not yet, but I was no longer dying.

At 11:00 p.m., I stood up and spent the next two hours wandering the cold and dark University of Michigan campus. How could I make sense of this experience? I was long gone from Judaism, which in any event no longer emphasizes personal experiences with God: how terribly arrogant to say that God, for some reason, had communicated personally with someone like me. Talk about it with professors and fellow U of M students? They'd think I was crazy.

I bounced past the Michigan Union, off the Literature, Science, and Arts building, past Angell Hall, off the Hatcher Graduate Library, nothing but *nyet*—a firm no to the atheist and Marxist vegetation that had grown in me for ten years. But what now? I was spiritually adrift. To keep this account short, I'll skip by my confused steps during the last two months of 1973 and note two books in 1974 that influenced me.

The first was a copy of the New Testament in Russian that a person in Oregon had given me: I had held onto it because it seemed exotic and it might be useful for reading practice. With a Russian-English dictionary in front of me I dived into the Gospel according to Matthew, chapter one. "The book of the genealogy of Jesus Christ, the son of David, the son of Abraham." I could understand that, and was delighted to find chapter one easy going: in the second verse Abraham begat Isaac, and other begats loped down the page.

Then came the Christmas story I had never read, followed by a massacre of babies, and John the Baptist's hard-hitting words: "You brood of vipers." It held my attention, and after a while I didn't punctuate the verses with sneers. Needing to read slowly and think about the words was helpful. The Sermon on the Mount impressed me. All the Marxists I knew were pro-anger, devoted to fanning proletarian hatred of The Rich. Jesus, though, was not only anti-murder but anti-anger: "Everyone who is angry with his brother will be liable to judgment." Marxists were "two eyes for an eye," but Jesus spoke of loving enemies and turning the other cheek.

Later that year I read *The American Puritans: Their Prose and Poetry*, edited by Perry Miller. The only reason I picked it up was because my Michigan fellowship required me in year two to teach an American Culture course. No professor wanted to teach about dead white males, but Early American Literature (largely Puritan sermons) was still in the course catalogue. I could not turn down the assignment, so I needed to cram.

The little I knew of Christian thought came largely from my observation of Boston Catholicism, heavy on ritual. The Puritans were different: They believed God is the agent of conversion and regeneration, with humans responsive yet not leading the process. God does not ticket for heaven those with good social conduct. Rather, God saves those he chooses to save regardless of their acts. Salvation then leads to better conduct.

That was good news for me. I had broken each of the Ten Commandments, except literally the prohibition of murder (but Jesus called anger a form of murder). I certainly was glad that God, if he were anything like the Puritans described him, would not judge me by my works. I assigned to students Thomas Hooker's sermon "A True Sight of Sin" in which Hooker described our insistence on autonomy: "I will be swayed by mine own will and led by mine own deluded reason." That was my history, and Hooker seemed to be preaching to me.

Still, I certainly did not want to be a Christian. I did not want to conform to its sexual standards, and I knew that a public commitment to Christ would hinder my academic career. I'll skip by other stones in the road in 1975 and 1976, and cut to what happened in the fall of 1976, when I was newly married and newly employed at San Diego State University. It seemed time not just to read books but to go to church. Using the yellow pages, and knowing from my reading that Christians baptized, I saw a long list under the "Churches—Baptist" heading.

Within that category was a subheading, "Conservative Baptist." I didn't want to attend a Marx-sympathizing church, so "conservative" sounded fine—and one small one was a few blocks away. The stucco building of First Baptist Church of La Mesa included a plain sanctuary with a stained glass window and a big baptistery behind the pulpit: Curtains shielded the baptizing tank from the rest of the sanctuary, and for three months I didn't know it was there because the curtain never opened. That's because church members were gray-haired, with the exception of a young pastor and his wife, who were polyestered like the rest of the congregation.

Pastor John Burger preached the same well-worn sermon every week, "Ye Must Be Born Again." We sang the same hymn, "Just as I Am," from well-worn hymnals. Normally I would respond condescendingly to such repetition, but the sermon and the song were exactly what I needed. Burger explained that we could not act rightly under our own power and that the Holy Spirit had to change us, that we'd know this was happening when we turned our lives around for reasons we hardly understood, and started thinking and acting in ways contrary to those the dark world around us emphasized.

Despite our cultural differences, this connected. I had learned I was powerless on my own. Good intentions did not last. Only God could give me the power to sin less. Burger stressed that only God could forgive me when I did, for the sake of Christ who died for me.

On All Saints Day, November 1, 1976, three years after God turned my life around, the church's deacon of visitation, elderly Earl Atnip, came to our apartment in La Mesa. He and I sat outside in the southern California sunshine. A simple, kind man with at most a high school diploma, he did not offer any intellectual razzamatazz. He held up a Bible and said, "You believe this stuff, don't you?" I mumbled, "Well, yeah, I do." He said, "Then you'd better join up."

Irrefutable logic—and I did join up, publicly professing faith in Christ and being baptized. The odds against my doing that, from a Jewish, Marxist, and academic background, were incredibly high, humanly speaking. But I had the sense, and not for the first or last time, that this had been predestined. Subjectively, I make choices from moment to moment. Objectively, I'm an actor, and God is the director. It's now forty-five years later, and my gratitude to God keeps growing. He's given me a good marriage and a good career, including three decades of editing *World*. To God be the glory.

# Partial Bibliography

Baron, Salo W. *The Russian Jew under Tsars and Soviets.* 2nd ed. New York: Macmillan, 1976.

Brown, Dwier. *If You Build It . . . : A Book about Fathers, Fate and Field of Dreams.* Ojai, CA: Elsie Jean Books, 2014.

Crews, Frederick. *Freud: The Making of an Illusion.* New York: Metropolitan Books, 2017.

Darwin, Charles. *The Descent of Man.* New York: Penguin Classics, 2004.

Freud, Sigmund. *The Future of an Illusion.* New York: W. W. Norton, 1989.

Hentoff, Nat. *Boston Boy.* 2nd ed. Philadelphia: Paul Dry Books, 2001.

Hochschild, Adam. *Half the Way Home: A Memoir of Father and Son.* New York: Viking, 1996.

Hooton, Earnest Albert. *Apes, Men, and Morons.* New York: G.P. Putnam's Sons, 1937.

———. *Up from the Apes.* Rev. ed. New York: Macmillan, 1946.

———. *Why Men Behave Like Apes.* Princeton, NJ: Princeton University Press, 1940.

Kaplan, Mordecai M. *Judaism as a Civilization: Toward a Reconstruction of American-Jewish Life.* New York: Macmillan, 1934.

Kaufmann, Yehezkel. *The Religion of Israel.* New York: Schocken, 1972.

Kemelman, Harry. *Friday the Rabbi Slept Late.* New York: Open Road Media, 2015.

———. *Sunday the Rabbi Stayed Home.* New York: Open Road Media, 2015.

Keyes, Ralph, ed. *Sons on Fathers: A Book of Men's Writing.* New York: HarperCollins, 1992.

Klayman, Richard. *A Generation of Hope: 1929–1941.* Malden, MA: Old Suffolk Square Press, 1987.

Munroe, Jeffrey. *Reading Buechner: Exploring the Work of a Master Memoirist, Novelist, Theologian, and Preacher.* Downers Grove, IL: InterVarsity Press, 2019.

Potash, Robert A. *Looking Back at My First Eighty Years.* New York: iUniverse, 2008.

Reuben, Steven. *A Year with Mordecai Kaplan: Wisdom on the Weekly Torah Portion.* Lincoln: University of Nebraska, 2019.

Sarna, Jonathan D., Ellen Smith, and Scott-Martin Kosofsky, eds. *The Jews of Boston.* Rev. ed. New Haven, CT: Yale University Press, 2005.

Scult, Mel, ed. *Communings of the Spirit: The Journals of Mordecai M. Kaplan,* Vol. 3, *1942–1951.* Detroit: Wayne State University Press, 2020.

Trillin, Calvin. *Messages from My Father.* New York: Farrar, Straus and Giroux, 1997.

Tromly, Frederic B. *Fathers and Sons in Shakespeare: The Debt Never Promised.* Toronto: University of Toronto Press, 2010.

Vaillant, George E. *Triumphs of Experience: The Men of the Harvard Grant Study.* Cambridge: Belknap Press, 2015.

Wells, H. G. *The Outline of History: Being a Plain History of Life and Mankind.* Rev. ed. Edited by Raymond Postgate and G. P. Wells. New York: Doubleday, 1971.

White, Theodore H. *In Search of History: A Personal Adventure.* New York: Warner, 1979.

**Marvin Olasky** (PhD, University of Michigan) is editor in chief of *World* and the author of twenty-eight books, including *Reforming Journalism* and *The Tragedy of American Compassion*. He is also dean of the World Journalism Institute and an elder in the Presbyterian Church in America. He was a *Yale Daily News* and *Boston Globe* reporter, wrote a syndicated column, and taught journalism and history for twenty-five years at The University of Texas at Austin. He has been married for forty-five years and has four sons.

Did you like this book?
Consider leaving a review online.
The author appreciates your feedback!

Or write to P&R at editorial@prpbooks.com
with your comments. We'd love to hear from you.